W9-BNP-297

GRAPHIC DESIGN
THINKING:
BEYOND BRAINSTORMING

Ellen Lupton, editor

Princeton Architectural Press, New York

Maryland Institute College of Art, Baltimore

Design Briefs—essential texts on design.
Also available in this series:
Designing for Social Change, Andrew Shea, 978-1-61689-047-6
D.I.Y. Design It Yourself, Ellen Lupton, 978-1-56898-552-7
Elements of Design, Gail Greet Hannah, 978-1-56898-329-5
Form+Code, Reas, McWilliams, & LUST, 978-1-56898-937-2
Geometry of Design, 2nd edition, Kimberly Elam, 978-1-61689-036-0
Graphic Design Theory, Helen Armstrong, 978-1-56898-772-9
Grid Systems, Kimberly Elam, 978-1-56898-465-0

Indie Publishing, Ellen Lupton, 978-1-56898-760-6
Lettering & Type, Bruce Willen & Nolen Strals, 978-1-56898-765-1
Participate, Armstrong & Stojmirovic, 978-1-61689-025-4
Thinking With Type, 2nd edition, Ellen Lupton, 978-1-56898-969-3
Typographic Systems, Kimberly Elam, 978-1-56898-687-6
Visual Grammar, Christian Leborg, 978-1-56898-581-7
The Wayfinding Handbook, David Gibson, 978-1-56898-769-9

Design Briefs Series Editor
Ellen Lupton

Published by
Princeton Architectural Press
37 East Seventh Street
New York, New York 10003

For a free catalog of books, call 1-800-722-6657.
Visit our website at www.papress.com.

© 2011 Princeton Architectural Press
All rights reserved
Printed and bound in China
14 13 12   4 3 2   First edition

No part of this book may be used or reproduced in any manner
without written permission from the publisher, except in the context
of reviews.

Every reasonable attempt has been made to identify owners of
copyright. Errors or omissions will be corrected in subsequent
editions.

Graphic design thinking : beyond brainstorming / edited by
Ellen Lupton.
1st ed.
p. cm.
Includes index.
ISBN 978-1-56898-979-2 (alk. paper)
1. Graphic arts—Technique. 2. Creative thinking.
I. Lupton, Ellen. II. Title.
NC997.L875 2011
741.6—dc22
                                    2010050679

Editor, Princeton Architectural Press
Linda Lee

Book Design, Maryland Institute College of Art
Lauren P. Adams, Christina Beard, Christopher Clark, Elizabeth
Anne Herrmann, Ann Liu, Ellen Lupton, Chris McCampbell, Jennifer
Cole Phillips, Virginia Sasser, Ryan Shelley, Wesley Stuckey, Beth
Taylor, Isabel Uria, Supisa Wattanasansanee, Krissi Xenakis

Art Direction/Style Police
Lauren P. Adams, Molly Hawthorne, Ann Liu

Cover Design
Lauren P. Adams (front), Ann Liu (back)

Visiting Artists
Oriol Armengou, Andrew Blauvelt, Denise Gonzales Crisp,
Luba Lukova, Debbie Millman, Ferran Mitjans, Georgianna Stout,
Martin Venezky

Typography
Berthold Akzidenz-Grotesk, 1896; VAG Rounded, 1979

This project was initiated by Maryland Institute College of Art's
Center for Design Thinking.

Special thanks to: Bree Anne Apperley, Sara Bader, Nicola
Bednarek Brower, Janet Behning, Megan Carey, Becca Casbon,
Carina Cha, Tom Cho, Penny (Yuen Pik) Chu, Russell Fernandez,
Jan Haux, John Myers, Katharine Myers, Margaret Rogalski, Dan
Simon, Andrew Stepanian, Jennifer Thompson, Paul Wagner,
Joseph Weston, and Deb Wood of Princeton Architectural Press
—*Kevin C. Lippert, publisher*

Contents

Introduction

The design process is a mix of intuitive and deliberate actions. Starting a project can include personal rituals like a long walk or a hot shower, or structured endeavors like interviewing the client or distributing a questionnaire. Many designers begin with *brainstorming*, an open-ended search for initial ideas that helps refine the problem and broaden how one thinks about it.

Brainstorming, invented in the 1950s, quickly became a popular way to help people think creatively—even people who don't consider themselves creative at all. Brainstorming remains a powerful tool, but it is just the beginning in a designer's quest for useful and inspiring ideas. This book explores over two dozen methods for thinking and making, organized around the three main phases of the design process: defining problems, getting ideas, and creating form. You can mix, match, and adapt these techniques to fit the projects and personalities at hand.

Nearly any person can learn to improve his or her creative abilities. Talent may be a mysterious entity, yet the creative process tends to follow predictable pathways. By breaking down this process into steps and implementing conscious methods of thinking and doing, designers can open their minds to vibrant solutions that satisfy clients, users, and themselves.

Design is a messy endeavor. Designers generate countless ideas that don't get used. They often find themselves starting over, going backward, and making mistakes. Successful designers learn to embrace this back-and-forth, knowing that the first idea is rarely the last and that the problem itself can change as a project evolves.

This book reflects the diversity of contemporary graphic design practice. Designers today work in teams to address social problems and business challenges. They also work individually to develop their own visual languages through the creative use of tools and ideation techniques. In classroom settings, design training tends to emphasize personal development, owing to the structure of schools and the expectations of students. In the workplace, however, collaboration is the norm, demanding designers to continually communicate with clients, users, and coworkers. The exercises featured in this book include team-based approaches as well as techniques that help designers expand their individual creative voices.

"Once a new idea springs into existence it cannot be unthought. There is a sense of immortality to a new idea."

Edward de Bono

The concept "design thinking" commonly refers to the processes of ideation, research, prototyping, and user interaction. Alex F. Osborn's *Applied Imagination* (1953) and Edward de Bono's *New Think* (1967) helped explain and popularize methods of creative problem solving. *The Universal Traveler*, published by Don Koberg and Jim Bagnall in 1972, presented readers with numerous ways to embark on the nonlinear path to problem solving. Peter G. Rowe applied the term design thinking to architecture in 1987. More recently, Tom Kelley, Tim Brown, and their colleagues at the design firm IDEO have developed comprehensive techniques for framing problems and generating solutions, emphasizing design as a means for satisfying human needs.

While some of these approaches encompass design in the broadest sense, our book focuses on graphic design—as a medium and as a tool. Ideation techniques often involve capturing ideas visually: making sketches, compiling lists, diagramming relationships, and mapping webs of associations. All of these modes of inquiry are forms of graphic expression—a point made in Dan Roam's excellent book *The Back of the Napkin* (2008). Designers of products, systems, and interfaces use narrative storyboards to explain how goods and services function.

In addition to presenting techniques for framing problems and generating ideas, this book looks at form-making as an aspect of design thinking. Whereas some advocates of design thinking de-emphasize the formal component of design, we see form-making as a crucial element of the creative process.

This book was authored, edited, and designed by students and faculty in the Graphic Design MFA program at Maryland Institute College of Art (MICA). *Graphic Design Thinking: Beyond Brainstorming* is the fifth in a series of books published by Princeton Architectural Press in collaboration with MICA's Center for Design Thinking. Producing these books helps students and faculty expand their own knowledge of design while sharing ideas with a community of designers and creative people working around the world. Our classrooms are practical laboratories, and these books are the results of our research. *Ellen Lupton*

WORKS CITED

Brown, Tim. *Change by Design: How Design Thinking Transforms Organizations and Inspires Innovation.* New York: Harper Business, 2009.

Buxton, Bill. *Sketching User Experiences: Getting the Design Right and the Right Design.* San Francisco: Morgan Kaufmann, 2007.

De Bono, Edward. *New Think: The Use of Lateral Thinking in the Generation of New Ideas.* New York: Basic Books, 1967.

Kelley, Tom, and Jonathan Littman. *The Art of Innovation: Lessons in Creativity from IDEO, America's Leading Design Firm.* New York: Random House, 2001.

Koberg, Don, and Jim Bagnall. *The Universal Traveler: A Soft-Systems Guide to Creativity, Problem-Solving, and the Process of Reaching Goals.* San Francisco: William Kaufmann, 1972.

Rowe, Peter G. *Design Thinking.* Cambridge: MIT Press, 1987.

Osborn, Alex F. *Applied Imagination: Principles and Procedures of Creative Thinking.* New York: Scribner's, 1953.

Roam, Dan. *The Back of the Napkin: Solving Problems and Selling Ideas with Pictures.* New York: Portfolio, 2008.

Brainstorming

Mind Mapping

Interviewing

The Design Process

This chapter follows one real-world project through each phase of the design process, from researching the problem to generating ideas to creating form. Along the way, the design team employed various techniques of design thinking that are explored in more detail later in the book. The project was conducted by students in the Graphic Design MFA program at MICA. A team of designers, led by Jennifer Cole Phillips, worked with client Charlie Rubenstein in an effort to raise awareness of homelessness in the local community. Knowing that they could not address all aspects of homelessness in a single project, the team worked to narrow their scope and create a project that could be successfully realized with available resources.

In 2008 Baltimore City documented 3,419 homeless people living within its limits. The team built their campaign around the number 3419, signaling both the scale of the problem and the human specificity of the homeless population. Working in conjunction with the client, the design team conceived and implemented a project that aimed to educate middle school students about homelessness. *Ann Liu*

"The design process, at its best, integrates the aspirations of art, science, and culture"

Jeff Smith

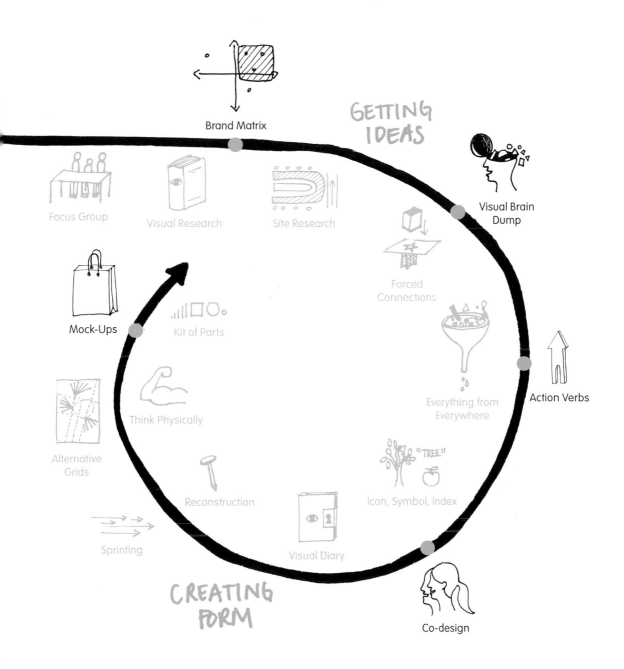

Brand Matrix

GETTING IDEAS

Visual Brain Dump

Focus Group

Visual Research

Site Research

Forced Connections

Action Verbs

Mock-Ups

Kit of Parts

Everything from Everywhere

Alternative Grids

Think Physically

"TREE"

Icon, Symbol, Index

Reconstruction

Sprinting

Visual Diary

CREATING FORM

Co-design

Defining
the Problem

Interview with Charlie Rubenstein

Interviewing. Designers talk to clients and other stakeholders to learn more about people's perceived wants and needs. Shown here are highlighted excerpts from a videotaped conversation with Charlie Rubenstein, the chief organizer of the 3419 homeless awareness campaign. *See more on Interviewing, page 26.*

Paired with his body language, Charlie's comments showed that he was dissatisfied with the current state of homeless services but also recognized their value.

Here, Charlie started talking more quickly and with more animation in his tone and body language, indicating his passion for treating homeless people like real people instead of just a number.

People often need time to get to the bottom line. After forty-five minutes, we were finally able to hear the core of what the client was trying to achieve with the 3419 campaign.

If we are talking about 3419 as an organization, where do you see it five years from now?
Well, I want to redesign the way we treat homelessness in the city. I don't want to do it from a nonprofit, third party level, I want to do it from the inside out.

My biggest problem with Baltimore's homeless services, or whatever you want to call it, is that they don't go very deep. There isn't enough reach. For me, it isn't that they are doing it wrong, there just needs to be a new way to do it.

Can you give me a specific example of a new way?
Sure. There needs to be more qualitative research done. There are more quantitative studies around than you could read in a lifetime....So, if you have a policy, its biggest problem is that it's singular and won't work for everybody. The biggest problem is that, even institutionally, we are treating people as numbers. We are treating people as a genre, as if they are faceless, heartless. Like they are just 3419.

I want to create a people-based program. Because we are talking about people, and there are so many different kinds of them. So, what if we tried to understand who each of these people are? Where they came from and what their names are...I want to do a six-month qualitative research study where we actually go out and interview over five hundred homeless people. And not just one time but over a period of time, so we can understand who these people are.

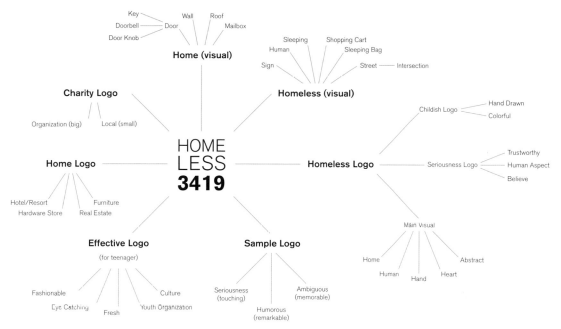

Mind Mapping. Designers use associative diagrams to quickly organize possible directions for a project. Design: Christina Beard and Supisa Wattanasansanee. *See more on Mind Mapping, page 22.*

CAN	WANT	ARE
WALK	BE HAPPY	MUSICIANS
WORK	BE SAFE	ARTISTS
SMILE	SUCCEED	VETERANS
FEEL		WORKERS

Brand Matrix. This diagram shows relationships among different social change campaigns. Some are single events, while others take place continuously. Some happen online, others, in person. *See more on Brand Matrix, page 42.*

Brainstorming. By focusing the campaign on what homeless people have and not what they materially lack, designers chose "can," "want" and "are" as the voice of the project. *See more on Brainstorming, page 16.*

Getting Ideas

Action Verbs. A fun way to quickly produce visual concepts is to apply action verbs to a basic idea. Starting with an iconic symbol of a house, the designer transformed the image with actions such as magnify, minify, stretch, flatten, and dissect. Design: Supisa Wattanasansanee. *See more on Action Verbs, page 74.*

Visual Brain Dumping. Designers created various typographic treatments of 3419 and grouped them together in order to find the best form for the project. Design: Christina Beard, Chris McCampbell, Ryan Shelley, Wesley Stuckey. *See more on Visual Brain Dumping, page 62.*

Creating Form

Collaboration. The stencil form was shared with a different team of designers to explore ways that users could transform it. Design: Paige Rommel, Wednesday Irotto, Hannah Mack. *See more on Collaboration, page 92.*

3419

Original DIN Bold

3419

Simplified visual weight

3419

Modified for stencil

Mock-Ups. Making visual mock-ups showing how concepts, like a pillowcase poster, could be applied in real life helps make it concrete for clients and stakeholders. Design: Lauren P. Adams. *See more on Mock-Ups, page 136.*

Ready for Reproduction. Having decided that a stencil would be part of the 3419 identity, the designer modified letters from the typeface DIN to create a custom mark that could function as a physical stencil. Design: Chris McCampbell.

The Whole Kit and Kaboodle. Designers created a poster and worksheets to teach kids about homelessness in Baltimore and what they can do to help. The kit also includes two stencils, two pillowcases, a bottle of paint, and a brush. The kit invites students to create their own pillowcase posters, engaging them actively in thinking about the problem and what it means to go to sleep without your own bed. Design: Lauren P. Adams, Ann Liu, Chris McCampbell, Beth Taylor, Krissi Xenakis.

The Cycle Continues

Design is an ongoing process. After a team develops a project, they implement, test, and revise it. For the 3419 homeless awareness campaign, the end result of the initial design phase was a kit for use in middle schools. The kit allowed the project team to interact with their audience, while the users created their own visual contributions with the materials provided and thus expanded the project's language. The design process began all over again.

Co-design. The 3419 design team conducted an afternoon workshop with local middle-school students in order to create pillowcases that would be used as posters to hang around their school and city. Co-design involves users in the creative process. *See more on Co-design, page 96.*

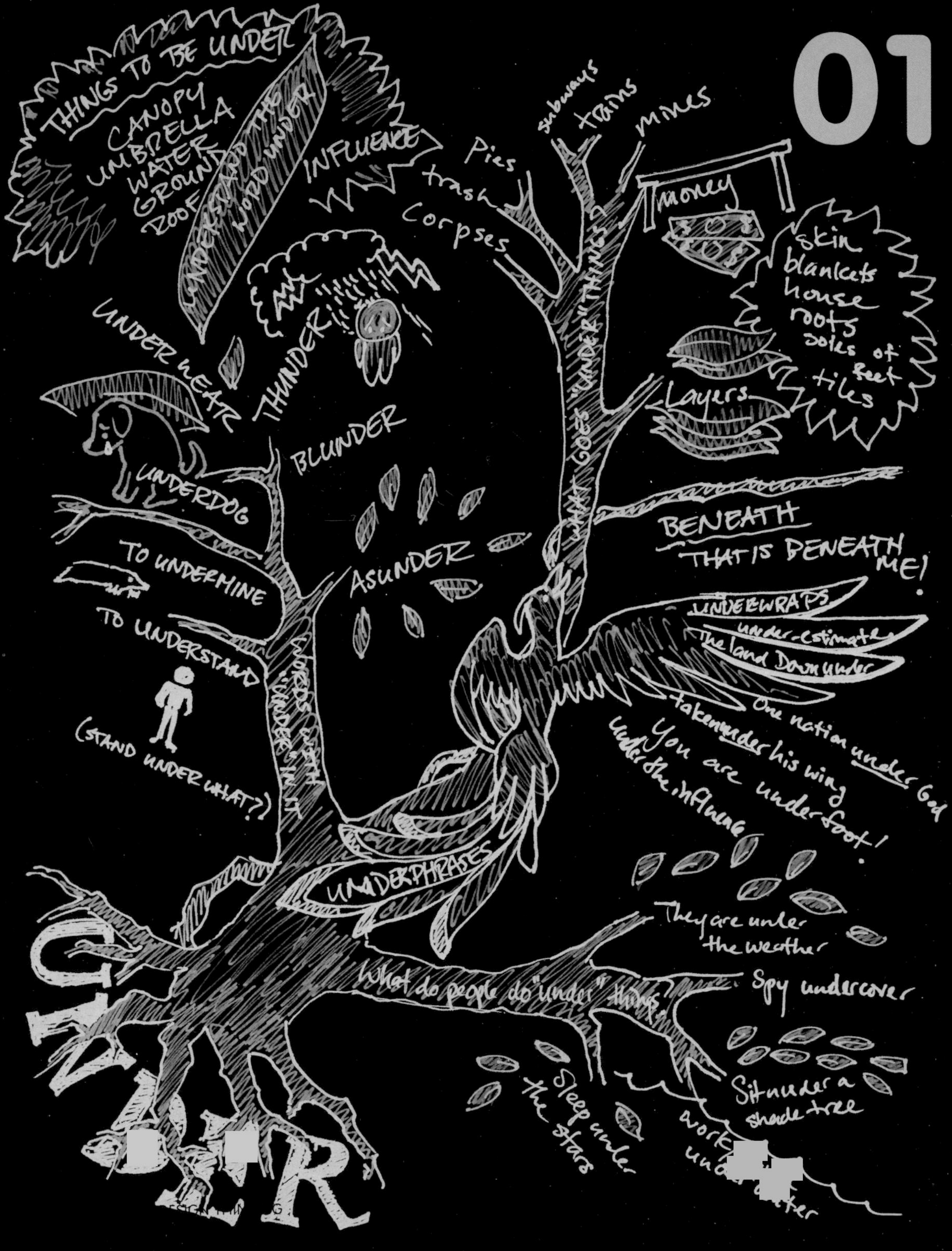

THINGS TO BE UNDER

CANOPY
UMBRELLA
WATER
GROUND
ROOF

UNDERNEATH THE WORD UNDER

INFLUENCE

Pies
trash
Corpses

subways
trains
mines

money
100

skin
blankets
house
roots
soles of feet
tiles

THUNDER

UNDER WEAR

BLUNDER

UNDERDOG

TO UNDERMINE

TO UNDERSTAND

(STAND UNDER WHAT?)

WHAT IS UNDER

Layers

ASUNDER

BENEATH
THAT IS BENEATH ME!

UNDERWRAPS
under-estimate
The land Down under
One nation under God
taken under his wing
You are underfoot!
under the influence

UNDERPHRASES

What do people do "under" things

They are under the weather

Spy undercover

Sleep under the stars

Sit under a shade tree

work under water

UNDER

01

"A problem well-stated
is half-solved."

John Dewey

How to Define Problems

Most design projects start with a problem, such as improving a product, creating a logo, or illustrating an idea. Designers and clients alike often think about problems too narrowly at the outset, limiting the success of the outcome. A client who claims to need a new brochure may do better with a website, a promotional event, or a marketing plan. A designer who thinks the client needs a new logotype may find that a pictorial icon or a new name will work better for a global audience. A search for greener packaging may yield not just individual products but new systems for manufacturing and distribution.

At the beginning of the design process, ideas are cheap and plentiful, pumped out in abundance and tossed around with abandon. Later, this large pool of ideas is narrowed down to those most likely to succeed. It takes time to visualize and test each viable concept. Thus, designers often begin with a period of playful, open-ended study. It's a process that includes writing lists as well as sketching images. It involves mapping familiar territory as well as charting the unknown.

This chapter looks at techniques designers use to define (and question) the problem in the early phases of the creative process. Methods such as brainstorming and mind mapping help designers generate core concepts, while others (such as interviewing, focus groups, and brand mapping) seek to illuminate the problem by asking what users want or what has been done before. Many of these techniques could take place at any phase of a project. Brainstorming is the first step in many designers' process, and it is the mother of many other thinking tools, so we put it at the beginning.

Why are such techniques—whether casual or structured—necessary at all? Can't a creative person just sit down and be creative? Most thinking methods involve externalizing ideas, setting them down in a form that can be seen and compared, sorted and combined, ranked and shared. Thinking doesn't happen just inside the brain. It occurs as fleeting ideas become tangible things: words, sketches, prototypes, and proposals. More and more, thinking happens among groups working together toward common goals.

Alex F. Osborn developed the technique of brainstorming in his book *Applied Imagination: Principles and Procedures of Creative Thinking*. (New York: Scribner's, 1953).

Brainstorming

What picture comes to your mind when you hear the word *brainstorm*? Many of us conjure a dark cloud crackling with lightning and raining down ideas. The original metaphor, however, was military, not meteorological. The term *brainstorming* was coined by Madison-Avenue ad man Alex F. Osborn, whose influential book *Applied Imagination* (1953) launched a revolution in getting people to think creatively. Brainstorming means attacking a problem from many directions at once, bombarding it with rapid-fire questions in order to come up with viable solutions. Osborn believed that even the most stubborn problem would eventually surrender if zapped by enough thought rays. He also believed that even the most rigid, habit-bound people could become imaginative if put in the right situation.

Today, brainstorming is deployed everywhere from kindergarten classrooms to corporate boardrooms. Brainstorming and related techniques help designers define problems and come up with initial concepts at the start of a project. These processes can yield written lists as well as quick sketches and diagrams. They are a handy way to open up your mind and unleash the power of odd-ball notions. *Jennifer Cole Phillips and Beth Taylor*

"The right idea is often the opposite of the obvious."

Alex F. Osborn

Photo: Christian Ericksen

How to Brainstorm in a Group

01 Appoint a moderator. Using a whiteboard, big pads of paper, or even a laptop, the moderator writes down any and all ideas. The moderator can group ideas into basic categories along the way. Although the moderator is the leader of the brainstorming process, he or she is not necessarily the team leader. Anyone with patience, energy, and a steady hand can do the job.

02 State the topic. Being specific makes for a more productive session. For example, the topic "new products for the kitchen" is vague, while "problems people have in the kitchen" encourages participants to think about what they do each day and what they might have trouble with. Breaking the topic down even further (cooking, cleaning, storage) can also stimulate discussion.

03 Write down everything, even the dumb stuff. Everybody in the group should feel free to put out ideas, without censorship. Unexpected ideas often seem silly at first glance. Be sure to record all the boring, familiar ideas too, as these help clear the mind for new thinking. Combine simple concepts to create richer ones.

04 Establish a time limit. People tend to be more productive (and less suspicious of the process) if they know the session won't drag on forever. In addition to setting a time limit, try limiting quantity (a hundred new ways to think about hats). Goals spur people on.

05 Follow up. Rank ideas at the end of the session or assign action steps to members of the group. Ask someone to record the results and distribute them as needed. The results of many brainstorming sessions end up getting forgotten after the thrill of the meeting.

Case Study
Designers Accord Summit

In the fall of 2009, the Designers Accord brought together one hundred global thought leaders for two days of highly participatory brainstorming, planning, and action around the topic of design education and sustainability. Valerie Casey, architect of the summit and founder of the Designers Accord, structured the event like a layer cake of short, small-group work sessions interspersed with lively lectures and opportunities for quality social time. The mix of activities helped prevent burnout and maximize productivity.

Participants worked in eight groups, and each group tackled the core challenge of the summit through a different lens. Groups rotated through the topics, allowing participants to refresh their perspectives and add to the collective wisdom of a larger endeavor. An efficient team of moderators and student assistants—plentifully equipped with Sharpies, Post-its, and whiteboards—kept conversations brisk and captured content along the way.

+ ─────── DEGREE OF DIVERGENT THINKING FROM THE CORE CHALLENGE ─────── +

LENS 1.
Reframe the topic to make it an answerable question or series of questions.

LENS 2.
Record everything that is known about the topic currently, and organize it.

LENS 3.
Freely ideate new approaches.

LENS 4.
Organize current information and new ideas. Strengthen and recombine. Select out weak ideas.

LENS 5.
Negate: list all the reasons these solution/s might not work.

LENS 6.
Strengthen the solution/s. Makes sure these solution/s are relevant to education and practice.

LENS 7.
Prototype/create a scenario of the ideal application of the solution.

LENS 8.
Clearly articulate the solution.

Social Brainstorming (above and opposite). Intense work sessions were interwoven with inspiring presentations and impromptu social gatherings. Moderators and student assistants worked to cultivate, capture, and cull ideas using every surface available: floors, walls, windows, and whiteboards. Photos: Christian Ericksen.

Through the Lens (left). A system of lenses for viewing the subject of sustainability and design education allowed for varying amounts of freedom and constraint. Diagram: Valerie Casey.

"Thinking Wrong is about breaking our own conventions or orthodoxies to generate as many solutions as possible, even if they seem 'wrong.'"

John Bielenberg

Case Study
PieLab

Designer John Bielenberg calls his unique design process Thinking Wrong. Using brainstorming and free association as jumping-off points, Bielenberg gets clients and design teams to hold a "blitz" at the start of a project. In a Thinking Wrong blitz, participants leave their assumptions at the door and generate as many ideas as possible. At the end of the blitz, wayward associations and seemingly random contributions often become the core of the design solution.

Bielenberg is the founder of Project M, an organization that inspires emerging designers to instigate social change. During a 2009 Project M session in Maine, the group found themselves halfway through their stay with no determined direction. To shake up the thinking process, Bielenberg asked the group about their respective talents. One participant's talent for baking pies led the team to wonder if homemade pies could become the center of a social action. The result was a forty-eight-hour public event called Free Pie. The project morphed into a pop-up shop called PieLab in Greensboro, Alabama, before becoming a permanent storefront there. Free Pie and PieLab are about more than baking. They bring people in the local community together to talk and share. As Bielenberg puts it, "Conversations lead to ideas, ideas to projects, and projects to positive change."

Recipe Invites. Design: Haik Avanian, Amanda Buck, Melissa Cullens, Archie Lee Coates IV, Megan Deal, Rosanna Dixon, Jeff Franklin, Dan Gavin, James Harr, Hannah Henry, Emily Jackson, Brian W. Jones, Reena Karia, Breanne Kostyk, Ryan LeCluyse, Robin Mooty, Alex Pines, Adam Saynuk, HERO staff and volunteers. Photo: Dan Gavin.

Come Together. Musicians from Sewanee University visit PieLab on opening day. Photo: Brian W. Jones.

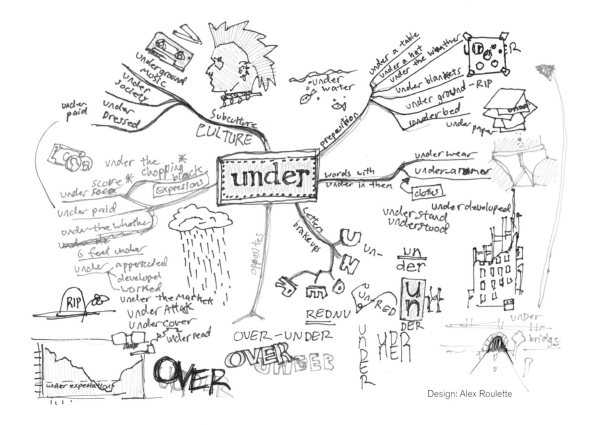

Design: Alex Roulette

Mind Mapping

Also called "radiant thinking," mind mapping is a form of mental research that allows designers to quickly explore the scope of a given problem, topic, or subject area. Starting with a central term or idea, the designer quickly plots out associated images and concepts.

Mind mapping was developed by Tony Buzan, a popular psychology author who has promoted his method through publications and workshops. Although Buzan delineated specific rules for mind mapping, such as using a different color for each branch of the diagram, his method is employed more loosely and intuitively by countless designers, writers, and educators. Ferran Mitjans and Oriol Armengou of Toormix, a design firm in Barcelona, call the technique "a cloud of ideas." *Krissi Xenakis*

On the theory of mind mapping, see Tony Buzan and Barry Buzan, *The Mind Map Book: How to Use Radiant Thinking to Maximize Your Brain's Untapped Potential* (New York: Plume, 1996).

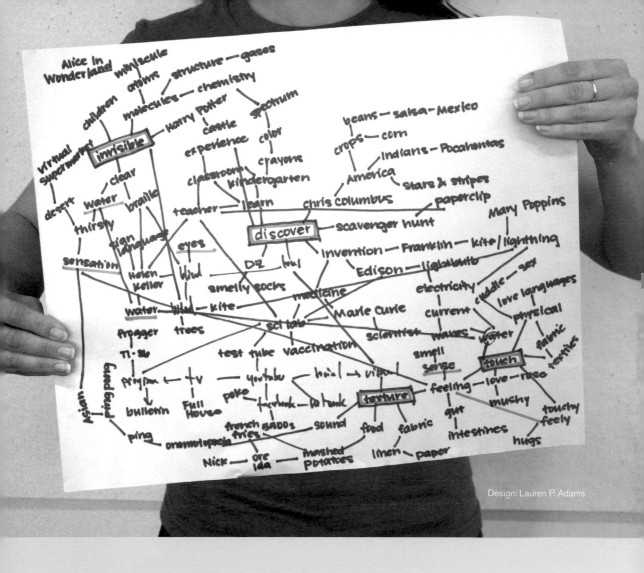

Design: Lauren P. Adams

How to Make a Mind Map

01 Focus. Place one element at the center of the page.

02 Branch out. Create a web of associations around the core phrase or image. If you like, use simple pictures as well as words.

03 Organize. The main branches of your map can represent categories such as synonyms, antonyms, homonyms, related compound words, clichés, stock phrases, and so on. Try using a different color for each branch you develop.

04 Subdivide. Each main branch can feed smaller subcategories. Work quickly, using the process to free up your mind. For example, the idea of discovery can take you from the names of inventors and inventions to the physical senses.

Case Study
Texturactiv Identity

During a two-day branding workshop, designers from Toormix encouraged a team of students to use mind mapping to develop a concept and naming system for a museum of textures. Toormix pushed the design team to keep searching for surprises.

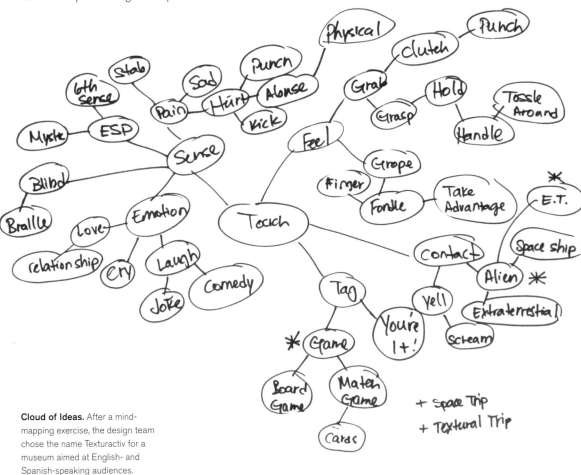

Cloud of Ideas. After a mind-mapping exercise, the design team chose the name Texturactiv for a museum aimed at English- and Spanish-speaking audiences. Design: Chris McCampbell.

A TACTILE EXPLORATORIUM

Image Solution. This logo incorporates photographs of real-world textures. The designer used geometric forms to represent a jungle gym and used the letterforms to frame an image of grass. Design: Beth Taylor.

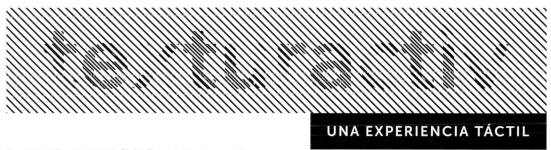

UNA EXPERIENCIA TÁCTIL

Expressing Touch through Sight. This solution draws on the words *invisible* and *waves*, concepts uncovered in the mind-mapping process. The stripes-on-stripes pattern undulates in and out of visibility, creating a visual texture. Design: Lauren P. Adams.

A TACTILE EXPERIENCE

Patterning. Many trails in the designer's mapping session led to the word *pattern*. She created a simple patterned background for the logotype. Elements of the pattern move in front of the lettering, generating a sense of depth. Design: Krissi Xenakis.

On ethnography as a design method, see Ian Noble and Russell Bestley, *Visual Research: An Introduction to Research Methodologies in Graphic Design* (West Sussex, UK: AVA Publishing, 2004) and Dev Patnaik, *Wired to Care: How Companies Prosper When They Create Widespread Empathy* (Upper Saddle River, NJ: FT Press, 2009).

Interviewing

Ethnography is the practice of gathering data through observations, interviews, and questionnaires. The goal of ethnographic research is to explore first-hand how people interact with objects or spaces. People aren't always good at verbally articulating what they want, but they can show it in their body language, their personal surroundings, and other subtle cues.

Field research involves going out into the participants' environment, observing them, asking them questions, and getting to know their concerns and passions. One-on-one interviewing is a basic form of field research. Taking part in direct observations and conversations helps connect designers to participants' behaviors and beliefs. Graphic designers can learn to use basic ethnographic field-research techniques to observe behavior patterns in an open and nonobtrusive way. This kind of research is especially useful when designing for unfamiliar audiences.

By applying a few key principles, the designer can lead an interview that yields valuable observations and content about users. Interviewing clients or users face-to-face, rather than via phone or email, allows the researcher to read body language and mood. By experiencing the same environment as the participant, the designer can begin to tease out new insights and gain empathy for the audience or user.

While the application of ethnographic research to graphic design is a relatively new idea, the basic principle of knowing who you are communicating with is a trademark of good design. *Ann Liu*

"What people say, what people do, and what they say they do are entirely different things."

Margaret Mead

How to Conduct an Interview

01 Find the right people.
Interview the people you'll be designing for. When identifying participants, look for users at the extreme end of the spectrum. If you're planning to design a productivity tool, you'll want to seek out highly organized participants as well as those who have never made a to-do list in their lives. Both will be able to provide enlightening field research.

02 Prepare, prepare, prepare.
Set up a video camera on a tripod if you'll be doing a sit-down interview. Make sure you have enough tape to cover the whole interview, and test your microphone ahead of time. Keep a notebook and pen handy to write notes for reference later.

03 What the heck? Look for moments when people are doing things differently from what they say they are doing. For example, if someone says they only keep the bare minimum of papers on their desk and you see overflowing stacks of files, you'll want to document that disconnect in your notes. It's these weird what-the-heck moments that allow you to see how everyday people think.

04 Be open. Be curious and look beyond the obvious. Coming into an interview with strong opinions won't allow you to see what your participants are trying to explain to you (or hoping to conceal). Try to step into the participants' shoes and understand why they're doing what you see them doing.

05 Silence is okay. Don't fill in the blanks. When your participants are pausing, they are thinking hard for the right word. Don't jump in and try to answer the question yourself. Patience can lead you to a great nugget of insight.

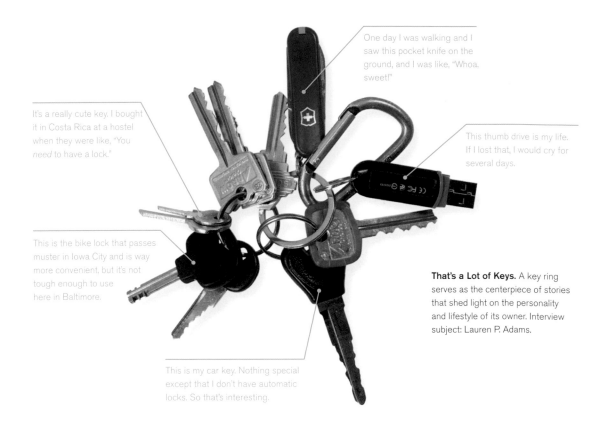

One day I was walking and I saw this pocket knife on the ground, and I was like, "Whoa, sweet!"

It's a really cute key. I bought it in Costa Rica at a hostel when they were like, "You *need* to have a lock."

This thumb drive is my life. If I lost that, I would cry for several days.

This is the bike lock that passes muster in Iowa City and is way more convenient, but it's not tough enough to use here in Baltimore.

That's a Lot of Keys. A key ring serves as the centerpiece of stories that shed light on the personality and lifestyle of its owner. Interview subject: Lauren P. Adams.

This is my car key. Nothing special except that I don't have automatic locks. So that's interesting.

Case Study
Key Interviews

The key is built into the everyday language of our lives. Kept close on a key chain and entrusted to loved ones, the key is iconic, utilitarian, and essential. Alas, it's become so familiar that people have forgotten its true worth. This interview is part of a research project studying the significance of keys as a designed artifact. Designer Ann Liu photographically documented sets of keys belonging to friends and identified points of interest through face-to-face interviews. She aimed to discover how someone's personality emerges from a description of his or her keys. The interviews led Liu to ask bigger questions about keys as significant and expressive objects.

Reporting from the Field.
This is an excerpt from an interview with a participant talking about each of her keys on her key ring.

Please tell me about each of your keys, and we'll follow through as needed.

Sure. This key with the teal markers is the one that gets me into my house.

Here?

Apartment! Apartment...commons...dorm room...let's be honest! [laughter] Which is why it has the teal ring on it; because it's important. These are the two keys to the offices where I work part-time. I can never tell them apart, and I haven't bothered to memorize the numbers.

Every time I try and get into one of the offices, I have to use both. I could try and learn it, and it would be so much easier, but...I don't spend the time. Or brainpower. What does this one go to? This is another office key. [whispers to self] Where does it go to? I don't even know...

The oldest thing on my keychain are all the key rings.
They're all from the first time I ever had a keychain. I keep really good track of them because I really like key rings that are loose so I can get the keys on and off. This one came with a keychain thing from high school. It was the ticket to my freshman-year high school sweetheart dance. The key ring was connected to some metal keychain thing that said, "A Night to Remember" or whatever. I threw that part away a long time ago—it had rhinestones in it! But, this is a good key ring, and it's not too tight and it's really big, and flat. So, I kept it.

Lauren, the interview subject, referred to her home as a house. The interviewer was confused about whether Lauren was referring to her house in her hometown or here on campus. A clarifying question quickly prompted Lauren to reiterate that she was now living in a dorm room. Her body language indicated that she felt slightly embarrassed that she had called her room a house.

Lauren asked herself a question out loud and paused to think. The interviewer sat quietly and let her look for the answer herself. After an extended pause, Lauren laughed and gave up. These keys (or the place they represent) may not be so important to her.

After the official interview had ended, Lauren continued to share snippets about her keys. The logic and sentimental origins of her key rings would have been lost if the recording had stopped at the end of the interview. Keep it rolling!

Focus Groups

The easiest ways to test the effectiveness of a design is to ask the intended audience what they think about it. A focus group is an organized conversation among a sample of individuals. Focus groups can be used to plan a project and define its goals as well as to evaluate results. Some designers avoid focus groups because they have seen clients use them to kill an idea before it even has a chance. If the questions are leading or if a few participants dominate the discussion and steer the opinion of the group, the results can damage the research. However, a focus group can yield helpful information if you conduct it carefully and interpret it with a degree of skepticism. Neither client nor designer should view the results as scientific evidence.

In addition to structured focus groups, designers can have spontaneous discussions with users—perhaps in a store or a public place. Helpful feedback often comes from a casual conversation that starts with the question, what does this mean to you? *Lauren P. Adams and Chris McCampbell*

"Focus groups are a somewhat informal technique that can help you assess user needs and feelings."

Jakob Nielsen

How to Conduct a Focus Group

01 Plan your questions.
What do you want to know? Plan to ask four or five questions in a two-hour session. Keep questions open-ended and neutral. Instead of asking, did you like the exhibition? ask, what do you remember from the exhibition?

02 Assign a moderator and assistant moderator. The moderator leads the discussion and takes basic notes; the assistant moderator takes comprehensive notes and makes sure the audio recording equipment is working before and during the event.

03 Create a comfortable environment. Request consent from participants to conduct the focus groups and inform them of how their responses will be used. Provide refreshments. Arrange participants in a circle. Keep to your time limit (no more than two hours).

04 Be open-minded. Don't lead the conversation toward a predetermined conclusion. If one participant is trying to convince other people to share his or her viewpoint, try to shift the direction of the conversation. Ask if anyone sees it differently.

05 Empower your participants.
Tell your group that they are the experts. Explain that you are there to learn about their opinions, experiences, and reactions.

06 Be supportive but neutral.
Ask, tell me more about that? or can you explain what you mean? or would you give me an example?

07 Ask one question at a time.
Repeat key phrases from your question to keep the conversation focused. Don't rush. Allow brief periods of silence while participants gather their thoughts.

Case Study
CARES Safety Center

The CARES Safety Center, created by Johns Hopkins Bloomberg School of Public Health Center for Injury Research and Policy, is a truck that travels to community events and schools in Baltimore and teaches children and their parents about injury prevention in the home. Some visitors reported feeling confused and overwhelmed by the interior of the truck and by the printed brochures. The CARES team joined forces with graphic designers from MICA's Center for Design Practice (CDP) to design clear, cohesive materials that are accessible to both English- and Spanish-speaking families. To inform the outcome of the new designs, the Johns Hopkins Bloomberg School of Public Health Center for Injury Research and Policy held focus groups with English- and Spanish-speaking parents.

What's Inside? At a focus group about a safety exhibition, the research team asked participants what they thought of the truck's exterior. Participants reported that they wanted to know what to expect inside the truck before entering. In response to this information, the designers created posters to place outside the safety center on sandwich boards. The posters explain in straightforward language that visitors will learn about home safety when they go inside the truck. Poster design: Andy Mangold. Project team: Lauren P. Adams, Mimi Cheng, Vanessa Garcia, Andy Mangold, Becky Slogeris.

LEARN ABOUT SAFETY IN YOUR HOME

CARES Safety Center

Fun, Free Exhibits
Low Cost Safety Products

RENDEN ERCA DE GURIDAD SU HOGAR

RES Centro de Seguridad

iciones Divertidos y Gratis
os Economicos de Seguridad

SAFETY CHECK
Steps to prevent injury in your home

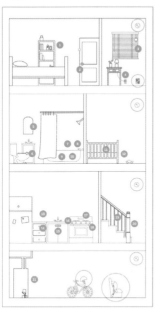

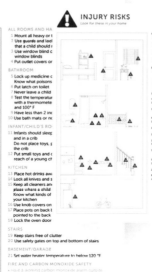

⚠ **INJURY RISKS**
Look for these in your home

ALL ROOMS AND HA

1. Mount all heavy or t
2. Use guards and latc
   that a child should n
3. Use window blind c
   window blinds
4. Put outlet covers on

BATHROOM

5. Lock up medicine c
   Know what poisons
6. Put latch on toilet
7. Never leave a child
8. Test the temperature
   with a thermomete
   and 100° F
9. Have less than 2 inc
10. Use bath mats or no

INFANT/CHILD'S RO

11. Infants should sleep
    and in a crib
    Do not place toys, p
    the crib
12. Put small toys and c
    reach of a young ch

KITCHEN

13. Place hot drinks aw
14. Lock all knives and s
15. Keep all cleaners an
    glass where a child
    Know what kinds of
    your kitchen
16. Use knob covers on
17. Place pots on back t
    pointed to the back
18. Lock the oven door

STAIRS

19. Keep stairs free of clutter
20. Use safety gates on top and bottom of stairs

BASEMENT/GARAGE

21. Set water heater temperature to below 120 °F

FIRE AND CARBON MONOXIDE SAFETY

- Have a working carbon monoxide alarm outside
  each sleeping area and on every level of
  your home
- Have a working smoke alarm outside each sleeping
  area and on every level of your home
- Make and practice a fire escape plan, with every
  member of the family

CAR SEAT AND BIKE SAFETY

- A child must be placed in a size-appropriate safety
  seat whenever riding in a car
- Helmets must be worn whenever riding a bicycle

ALL ROOMS AND HALLWAYS

1. Heavy or tall furniture not mounted to
   the wall can tip over
2. Some rooms in the home, like the bathroom
   and basement, should not be open to a child
   to get into alone
3. Window blind cords can strangle a child if
   the cords are loose
4. Electrical outlets can be dangerous if a child
   sticks objects (toys, fingers, etc.) into them

BATHROOM

5. Medicine cabinets may have many harmful
   products (medicines, beauty and hair care
   products)
6. Toilets can harm a child from falls or drowning
7. A child can drown or be injured in the bathtub
8. Bath water that is too hot can cause scald burns
9. A child can drown in just inches of water
10. Bathtubs can be slippery

INFANT/CHILDREN'S ROOM

11. Cribs or beds with pillows, loose blankets,
    or toys could suffocate a child
12. Small toys and objects can cause a young
    child to choke

KITCHEN

13. Hot drinks left on a counter or table can
    burn a child
14. Knives and other sharp objects left out
    on the open can be a cutting risk
15. Unlocked cabinets with cleaners and other
    products could be a poison risk
16. Stove and oven knobs can be turned on by a child
17. Pots and pans placed on front burners can
    be a burn risk for a child
18. Oven doors can be opened by a child and can
    cause the oven to tip over or burn the child

STAIRS

19. Clutter on the stairs can cause somebody
    to trip and fall
20. Stairs can cause serious fall injuries

BASEMENT/GARAGE

21. Water heater temperature set too high can cause
    scald burns

Rowhouse Relevance. Focus group participants explained that they wanted to see how the injury risks and safety checks shown in the exhibition relate to conditions in their own homes. In response, the design team created cross-sectional diagrams of a typical local rowhouse. Each numbered callout relates to a lesson taught at the CARES Safety Center. Design: Mimi Cheng.

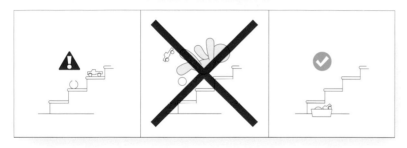

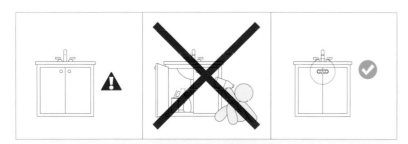

Icon System. To unify the visual language of the CARES Safety Center, the design team created icons that indicate injury risks and safety measures. Both focus groups (English- and Spanish-speaking) responded well to the icons, interpreting the meaning of the colors and forms correctly and consistently. The design team applied the icons to a series of diagrams that reinforce the lessons taught in the exhibition. Design: Andy Mangold.

Case Study
Baltimarket

A team of designers from MICA's CDP collaborated with the Baltimore City Health Department to address the problem of food access in the city. A "food desert" is an urban area that lacks convenient means to fresh food via a market or grocery store. A virtual supermarket initiative was launched to help combat the problem. This pilot project allows neighborhood residents to order groceries online at a local public library. The supermarket delivers the groceries to the library the following day with no delivery charge to the customers. The program provides people with convenient, varied food choices at standard supermarket prices. The designers' task was to create advertising collateral to promote and explain the program to area residents. But what was the best way to illustrate this unfamiliar service and complex issue? What imagery and language would be most clear? The design team created a poster and then talked to program participants about it when they came to the library. These were casual conversations rather than formal focus groups. The designers listened closely to what they heard—and then completely revised their approach.

Casual Feedback. In the beginning, the virtual-supermarket pilot program offered complimentary fresh fruit and vegetables in the library lobby. The designers used these short, casual encounters to ask questions about people's reaction to the initiative and to learn about their typical grocery-shopping behavior.

Bus Advertising. Most community members reported riding the bus to get to the grocery store, so bus advertising became a primary communications channel. Design: Lauren P. Adams.

Logo Development. The designers talked to community members about possible names for the virtual supermarket program. Many people liked Baltimarket because it is community specific. The main logo can be subtitled with the names of specific neighborhoods. Design: Lauren P. Adams.

Insulated Grocery Bags. Many customers complained that their frozen foods melted on the walk home from the library in the Baltimore summer heat. In response, the designers printed insulated reusable grocery bags as a customer incentive. Design: Lauren P. Adams.

Ordering groceries at a library is an unfamiliar activity. The text focuses on a simple action.

ORDER YOUR GROCERIES HERE.

**EASY ORDERING.
FREE DELIVERY.
CONVENIENT PICK UP.**

The design team opted for simple, straightforward language, believing that users were more likely to read a short poster than a detailed explanation.

The designers used colorful images of food and a brown bag to convey the idea of grocery shopping.

Eat fresh & live healthy, Baltimore.

The designers directly addressed Baltimore residents.

SEVERAL WAYS TO PAY

Next Ordering

Next Delivery

The designers left this section blank to allow the posters to be used at different times and locations.

SANTONI'S Supermarket

Virtual Supermarket Pilot, Round One. Before Baltimarket even had a name, the designers used this poster to generate feedback and create a more strategic, focused, and effective campaign. This initial poster focused on fresh food and the simple act of shopping. The designers didn't explain how the virtual supermarket process works, because they didn't know how the community would respond to the computer component of the program. Design: Lauren P. Adams and Chris McCampbell.

SUPERMARKET

— 1.4 MILES

YOUR NEAREST SUPERMARKET IS OVER ONE MILE AWAY.

MLK Jr Blvd

WASHINGTON VILLAGE LIBRARY

A *food desert* is a neighborhood without access to affordable, healthy food options.
YOU LIVE IN A FOOD DESERT.

An unhealthy diet is strongly linked to obesity, heart disease, and diabetes. How can you be expected to eat healthy without access to fresh food?

GET YOUR GROCERIES DELIVERED TO YOUR LIBRARY.

Ordering groceries from Santoni's Supermarket at the Washington Village Enoch Pratt Library is convenient. Delivery to the library is free. Pay with cash, credit, debit, or EBT/food stamps.

PAY WITH EBT, CASH, OR CREDIT

Order every Monday, 12 PM – 3 PM
Pick-up every Tuesday, 1 PM – 2 PM

For more information, contact the Baltimore City Health Department at 410-545-7544.

SANTONI'S *Supermarket*   ENOCH PRATT *free LIBRARY*

People were confused about the food imagery on the previous poster. They thought the initiative was about nutrition or farmers' markets. A map of the neighborhood makes the issue more personal to the target audience.

The primary message of the campaign shifted when the design team realized people were unaware of the underlying problem.

Using actual terminology empowers the audience to talk about the situation.

Because people were excited when they learned they could pay with food stamps, among other ways, the designers made this information more prominent.

The designers got positive feedback about the participation of the local grocery store, so they enlarged the sponsors' logos.

Virtual Supermarket Pilot, Round Two. Many visitors to the pilot program wanted to know why groceries were being sold at the library—people needed to understand the problem before they could engage with the solution. The second poster shifted emphasis from the specific program at the library to raising awareness about the issue. After further testing and feedback, the Baltimarket identity was established, and the message became a hybrid of the two pilot designs. Design: Lauren P. Adams and Chris McCampbell.

Quiksilver:

Quiksilver has developed from a 1970s boardshort company into a multinational apparel and accessory company grounded in the philosophy of youth. Our mission is to become the leading global youth apparel company; to maintain our core focus and roots while bringing our lifestyle message of boardriding, independence, creativity and innovation to this global community.

Individual expression, an adventurous spirit, authenticity and a passionate approach are all part of young people's mindset and are the essence of our brands. Combine this with the aesthetic appeal of beaches and mountains, and a connection is established that transcends borders and continents. Include thirty-plus years of quality, innovation and style, and you have Quiksilver.

Rip Curl:

Rip Curl is a company for, and about, the Crew on The Search. The products we make, the events we run, the riders we support and the people we reach globally are all part of the Search that Rip Curl is on.

The Search is the driving force behind our progress and vision. When Crew are chasing uncharted reefs, untracked powder or unridden rails, we want to arm them with the best equipment they'll need. No matter where your travels lead you, we'll have you covered.

Rip Curl will continue to stick by the grass roots that helped make us the market leader in surfing, but we'll also charge on in to the future and push riding to a new level.

Rip Curl: Built for riding and always searching for the ultimate journey...

Hurley:

The Essence of Hurley is based on our love of the ocean and its constant state of change. With deep roots in beach culture, we are all about inclusion and positivity. Our brand was started with the idea of facilitating the dreams of the youth. Music and art are the common threads that bring us all together. We are passionate about freedom of expression and the individual voice. We place a premium on smiles. Welcome to our world - imagine the possibilities.

Volcom:

The Volcom idea would incorporate a major philosophy of the times, "youth against establishment". This energy was an enlightened state to support young creative thinking. Volcom was a family of people not willing to accept the suppression of the established ways. This was a time when snowboarding and skateboarding was looked down on... Change was in the air.

It was all about spirit and creativity. Since those wild beginnings, the Volcom Stone has spread slowly across the world. The Company has matured internally but continues to run off the same philosophy it started with. The Volcom thinking now flows through its art, music, films, athletes and clothing....

Ideals of youth
Roots and authenticity
Globalization
Love of beaches, mountains, and the streets
Individual expression and creativity
Progression and adventure

Language Study
Design: 2x4

Visual Research

The renowned international design firm 2x4 uses visual research to analyze content, generate ideas, and communicate points of view. "We don't actually use the term *research*, because our method is qualitative. We prefer the term *speculation*," notes 2x4 partner Georgianna Stout. 2x4's speculative studies examine the conceptual space that a brand occupies by looking at the product from diverse, often contradictory, angles. In one such study, The Battle for Blue, 2x4 organized multinational corporations according to their proprietary colors, revealing overcrowding in the blue range and underdeveloped potential in pink and green. 2x4 has also analyzed the messages employed by sports companies in order to identify dominant themes and points of difference that could help distinguish a company from its competition. Explorations like these can become a foundation from which to create innovative, informed visual solutions. *Christina Beard*

"Many of 2x4's projects...are as much about the thinking process behind each work as the finished product."

Joseph Rosa

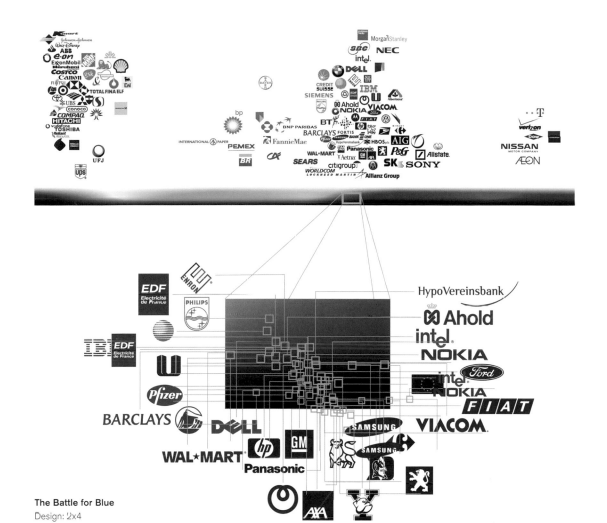

The Battle for Blue
Design: 2x4

How to Conduct Visual Research

01 Collect. Begin an open-ended study of the brand space of a particular client, product, or service. Look at logos, naming strategies, promotional language, color, and other aspects of the brand.

02 Visualize. Choose an area to analyze visually. Look for repetitive patterns and trends, such as recurring vocabulary, commonly used colors, or consistent product features.

03 Analyze. Draw insights from your data visualization. Does it suggest ways that your client or service could differentiate itself from the pack or assert leadership in a particular area?

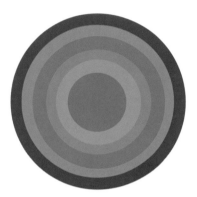

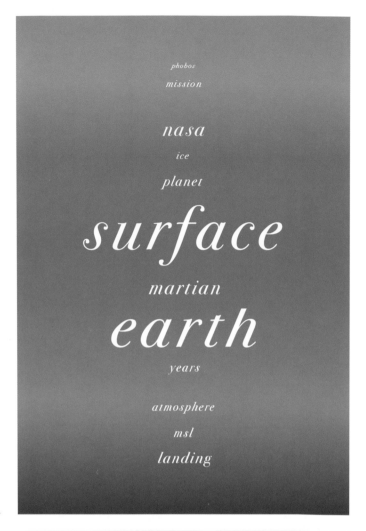

phobos
mission

nasa
ice
planet
surface
martian
earth
years
atmosphere
msl
landing

Mars Research. This visual study documents the colors used to represent Mars in scientific imagery. The designer developed color schemes by extracting average hues from hundreds of Mars-related images. She also chose commonly used words from texts describing Mars, both popular and scientific. Design: Christina Beard. Photos courtesy of NASA. Design research workshop led at MICA by Georgianna Stout, 2x4.

Key Study. Seeking to understand how keys are marketed and distributed, the designer collected photos of numerous keys and sorted them by shape, form, and color. Design: Ann Liu. Design research workshop led at MICA by Georgianna Stout, 2x4.

Brand Matrix Study (detail).
Art director: Debbie Millman

Brand Matrix

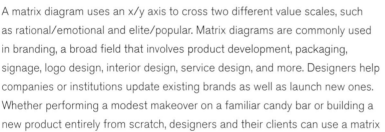

A matrix diagram uses an x/y axis to cross two different value scales, such as rational/emotional and elite/popular. Matrix diagrams are commonly used in branding, a broad field that involves product development, packaging, signage, logo design, interior design, service design, and more. Designers help companies or institutions update existing brands as well as launch new ones. Whether performing a modest makeover on a familiar candy bar or building a new product entirely from scratch, designers and their clients can use a matrix diagram to look at where their brand sits in relation to similar products or companies.

Brand mapping can be conducted with various levels of detail and formality. The process of making a brand map can draw out people's feelings about a specific product (say, a Ford Explorer) or about a broader category (SUVs). Designers use matrix diagrams to position brands according to categories such as name recognition, cost/value, prestige, safety, and market segment. Matrix diagrams help people visualize other kinds of content as well. Psychoanalysts and cultural anthropologists have used them to map the human psyche and social behavior, while *New York* magazine uses its weekly column "Approval Matrix" to map popular culture. *Krissi Xenakis*

"Market research is an art, not a science. Try to investigate emotional connections and design sensibilities."

Debbie Millman and
Mike Bainbridge

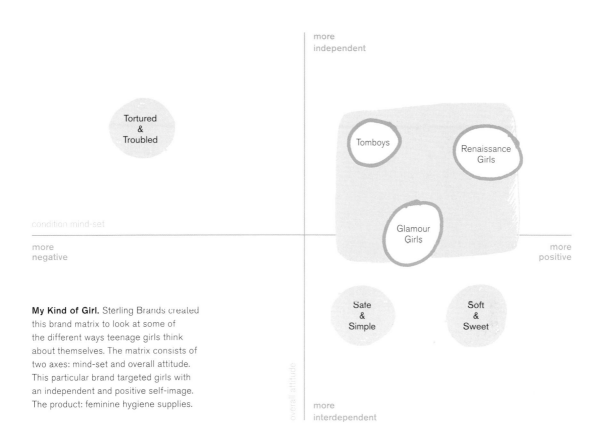

My Kind of Girl. Sterling Brands created this brand matrix to look at some of the different ways teenage girls think about themselves. The matrix consists of two axes: mind-set and overall attitude. This particular brand targeted girls with an independent and positive self-image. The product: feminine hygiene supplies.

How to Make a Brand Matrix

01 Get smart and start a list. Study the subject area you are seeking to understand. This could be a group of products, a user culture, a series of events, or a collection of objects or attributes. Create a list of elements to diagram. These elements could be brands, people, personalities, logos, products, etc. For example, the matrix above looks at attitudes of teenage girls.

02 Finding opposites. Make a list of polarities that you could use to organize your material, such as east/west, high/low, good/evil, formal/informal, expensive/cheap, fancy/plain, risky/safe, freedom/control, common/uncommon, etc. The diagram above looks at the relative independence of girls (as opposed to their reliance on a group) as well as their positive or negative outlooks.

03 Connect the dots. Plot the elements in your list on the matrix. Look for meaningful patterns in the results. Do items tend to cluster in one area? Is there an empty space that should be avoided, or is there a sweet spot you want to hit? The sweet spot in the diagram above encompasses girls who are independent and have a positive outlook.

Case Study
Tea Packaging Prototypes

Most people don't expect a carton of milk or a can of beans to be philosophical, but a box of tea often promotes ideas about wellness, world culture, relaxation, spirituality, and more. Indeed, tea can be a densely branded, message-heavy product, from the bag itself to the outer carton that contains it.

Shown here are proposals for new brands of tea that each have a strong visual identity. The designers studied the existing "brand space" of tea before developing new concepts. These prototypes draw on cultural ideas about the world's most popular beverage. Speaking to a range of emotions and desires, each of these brands stakes out its own place within the cultural matrix of tea.

Laid Back. This tea brand uses hand-drawn elements, natural colors, and matte materials to convey an updated hippie attitude. Design: Alex Roulette.

Tea Space. The matrix presented on the left maps the intersection of East/West and Formal/Informal.

Clean Cure. Many people view tea as a cleansing elixir. This brand responds with high-tech, pharmaceutically inspired graphics. Design: Cody Boehmig.

Upscale Eastern. This elegant prototype uses sleek contemporary graphics to celebrate the Eastern origins of tea. Design: Yu Chen Zhang.

Down Home. Drinking sweet tea from Mason jars is a favorite in the American South. Black Mountain is a historic town in North Carolina. Design: Julia Kostreva.

Asian American. This packaging combines Chinese characters with humorous illustrations to suggest Asian life in the American suburbs. Design: Tiffany Shih.

Brand Books

A brand book is a way to visualize the personality and life story of a product, company, or organization. The designer uses a selection of colors, shapes, textures, photographs, words, and photos to set a mood, inviting the reader to see and feel the product and to imagine it in the context of a lifestyle or human narrative. Often used to inspire brand loyalty and understanding, rather than to promote a specific product, brand books speak to people inside a company as well as to editors, investors, business partners, and consumers. They document the sources of inspiration behind a company or product, helping focus the brand around tangible images. A brand book can help a company understand itself as well as communicate its point of view to others. The design consultancy Wolff Olins created a brand book (above and opposite) for a competition to create a symbol for New York City. In addition to showing the proposed trademark, the book features inspirational shots of the five boroughs. *Ann Liu*

A brand book is about language, attitudes, and ideas more than it is about products.

The Spirit of the City. This brand book compiles images and commentary by famous New Yorkers that reflect the spirit of the city and the brand's inclusive, down-to-earth attitude. Design: Wolff Olins.

How to Make a Brand Book

01 Choose a format. Select an appropriate size. A big hardcover volume will feel like a deluxe coffee table book, while a modest 5 x 5 inch saddle-stitch notebook will feel casual and ephemeral. Is your brand an exclusive fashion label or a grassroots social organization? Choose formats and materials that reflect who you are.

02 Collect imagery. Look at everything that brought you to this point: inspirational images, sketches, printed pieces, text, photographs, patterns, fabric swatches. Starting with a diverse pool of materials will help you visualize an authentic brand.

03 Design and combine. The materials you collected might look like a pile of junk; your task is to communicate what each piece contributes to the world you are building. Making connections between images will help the visual language of the brand emerge.

04 Consider the pacing. Juxtaposing full-bleed photography with hand-drawn illustrations or scans of raw materials can provide a break from text-heavy pages. Control the mood. Is your book a constant barrage of photo collages, or does it provide the viewer with a zen moment at the turn of every page? Flipping through your brand book should help viewers imagine living with your product.

05 Make it real. The weight and feel of a real book gives presence to your brand. A brand book can be custom printed, handmade, or produced via a print-on-demand publishing service, depending on your resources.

Scintilla Stencils (above). A brand book can showcase real-life applications of a product. Well-crafted visuals help readers envision how a brand functions. The product line shown here is a kit of stamps and stencils for creating patterns. Design: Supisa Wattanasansanee.

Desoto Clothes (opposite). This brand book uses text that has been written with a Southern accent and photographs that were shot in natural surroundings to set the tone for a clothing line produced in the American South. Design: Wesley Stuckey.

Site Photos (left). To plan temporary signage for an urban aquarium, the designer took photos of the site, documenting several views of the environment for use in the design process.

Site Plan (opposite). The designer created a site plan with a notational layer that marks primary views and main traffic areas. Design: Chris McCampbell

Site Research

Signage and exhibition design incorporate techniques from architecture, industrial design, information design, and graphic design. Site research is essential to any project that exists in the built environment, immersing designers in the concrete constraints of a place. Actively observing a place is like setting up a campsite. Campers make active decisions and modifications to their location (just because there is grass on the ground does not mean a location is ideal). Likewise, by getting intimately acquainted with a built environment, designers gain the authority to say, this sign is too high, this one is hard to find, or this one doesn't belong.

Signs, textures, colors, sounds, surfaces, and structures all contribute to the built environment. Existing elements can obstruct views or distract visitors, but they can also provide unexpected opportunities. A column could hide a graphic element or block traffic, or it could provide a convenient surface for a sign. Think about the diverse populations that will use your signs and the environment: the Americans with Disabilities Act (ADA) sets standards for the accessibility of signs, while the local contexts suggest ideas about form or language use. Understanding the physical and social context is the starting point for environmental design. *Chris McCampbell, Ryan Shelley, and Wesley Stuckey*

Existing elements can obstruct views and distract visitors, but they can also provide unexpected opportunities.

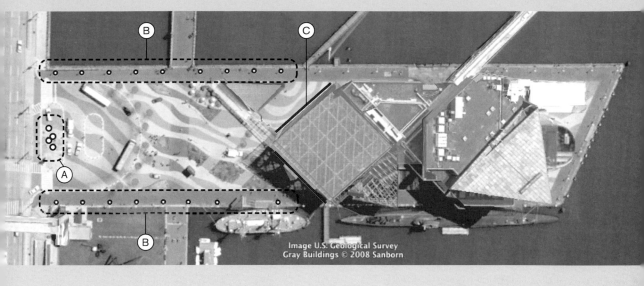

Image U.S. Geological Survey
Gray Buildings © 2008 Sanborn

How to Research a Site

01 Visit the site. The best way to think about a site is to go there. Visit the site at multiple times of day. Traffic fluctuations and lighting can change the space dramatically. Sketch out a plan where you can mark points of interest as well as potential problems.

02 Observe and photograph the site. Consider views and traffic from the standpoint of drivers and pedestrians. Where are you likely to enter or exit? What is the view from the street? Note landscaping or architectural features that could affect the project. Be critical of surrounding graphics or other signage that could cause confusion. Include elements such as cars and pedestrians in your photos to help

provide scale reference. Back at your work space, sort your photographs and notes, developing categories for different conditions and problems. You may see things in the photos that you didn't notice on location.

03 Create a site plan. Locate traffic patterns and primary views on a map of the area. (Google Maps and Google Earth are good resources.) The site plan will reveal zones that are overlooked or overworked. Locate proposed signage that is appropriate to the space and the amount of traffic. Consider the purpose of your signs: to identify, direct, or interpret buildings and spaces. Too many graphics could cause confusion while cluttering the landscape.

04 Trace photos of the site. Simplify your photographs by sketching over them and reducing the images to simple outlines. Include only what is needed to show the space. This editing process will allow you to analyze the environment and quickly explore concepts.

05 Sketch concepts. Use your traced photos to explore scale, placement, and relationships. Take advantage of existing architectural and natural features, such as grids, colors, textures, and lighting. These elements will add character and create a unity between your design and the space, helping people understand it better.

Case Study
National Aquarium

The National Aquarium is a major tourist destination located in Baltimore's Inner Harbor district. Visitors approach the facility by car, by boat, and on foot. Designer Chris McCampbell studied the site and proposed signage that promotes temporary exhibitions at the aquarium. He also proposed new directional signs inside the museum.

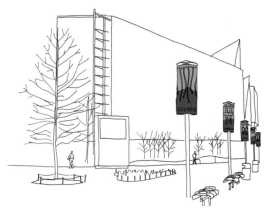

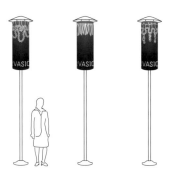

Tracing and Testing. Make simple line drawings by tracing your photographs. This allows you to develop quick concept sketches and experiment with placement.

Floor Plan. Sometimes a detailed floor plan is not readily available to the graphic designer. Sketch a plan of the space while you are on site and make notes of optimum views and potential sign locations.

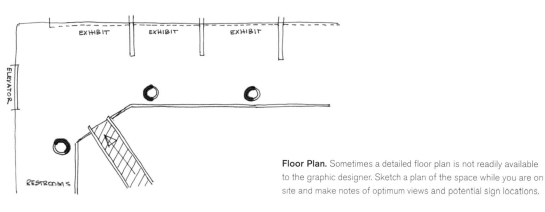

Clear the Way. A simple tracing allows you to eliminate distracting elements and compensate for poor lighting in your photographs.

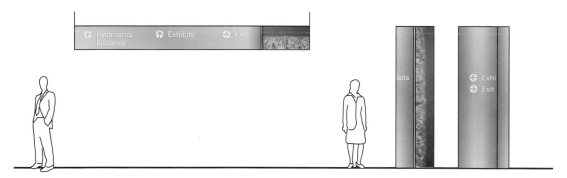

Formalize. More formal design proposals can be built from measurements and photographs collected on site.

Case Study
Baltimore Metro

Designers Ryan Shelley and Wesley Stuckey went on-site to document the Baltimore Metro's signage system. Traveling to every stop on the line, they photographed hundreds of signs in context. They looked at signs on platforms, inside trains, in stations, and on the street. When they returned to their studio, they printed out the photographs and arranged them on a pin-up wall in order to find problems, patterns, and inconsistencies within the system.

Old Systems. The lozenge-shaped signs are part of the current signage system, but an older system of rectangles is still in play, making the subway station appear poorly planned.

Vertically Challenged. An outdoor sign is visible from the platform, but the sign is placed too high to be seen easily from inside the subway car.

Overlap. Three different visual systems overlap at the entrance to this station. Only the freestanding pillar is from the current system. Additionally, this pillar, and many others, are missing a subway map.

Drowned Out. Signs are poorly integrated with the artwork that appears in some of the stations. Here, important directional signs get lost in the surrounding mural.

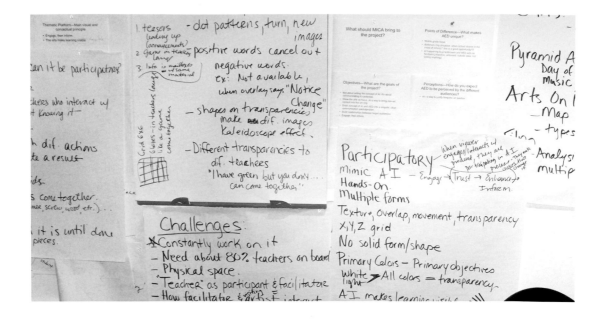

Creative Brief

Behind many successful design projects lie concrete and concise creative briefs. This jointly authored statement of goals requires the designer and client to invest time and consideration into the project at the outset. The creative brief, then, serves as a checkpoint for evaluating work as it progresses. MICA's CDP, a multidisciplinary studio that engages students in community-centered projects, developed a design process that uses the creative brief to inform every step of the design process, from generating concepts and conducting on-site research to producing complex advertising campaigns, exhibitions, and brand identities. The CDP team uses a questionnaire as a starting point to help clients articulate their project's goals. Then the designers use their own immersive research to modify and inform the client's initial brief. By combining the designers' research with client feedback, the team is able to collaboratively generate effective, focused solutions. *Lauren P. Adams*

"It is often better to ignore the client's brief and come back with a set of tough questions."

Erik Spiekermann

How to Refine a Creative Brief

01 Pose questions. Give the client a list of questions about the project. The answers will serve as the first draft of the creative brief. Potential questions include, what characteristics best describe your envisioned outcome? what makes your project unique? why do you believe your project will succeed? who is your audience? who will implement or maintain the project after it is launched?

02 Conduct research. Get to know your client and audience. Go on field trips and talk to strangers. Spend time exploring similar initiatives. What's been done before? In what environment will your project live? Is what you learn in line with your client's previous answers? Use your client as a partner. Update and refine your creative brief in response to what you have learned.

03 Narrow the brief. Using your client's input and your own research, define the essence of the project. Create a single sentence explaining the project's significant features.

04 Define key messages. List the main ideas the project needs to convey. Discuss the brief with your client. When all parties agree, start developing solutions that fit the project's goals.

Case Study
Arts Every Day

Arts Every Day is an organization that aims to make the arts an integral part of education in all Baltimore City schools. In the responses to a questionnaire from MICA's CDP, Arts Every Day requested a promotional piece to help teachers and administrators realize the importance of arts integration in their curricula. To learn about its audience, the CDP designers spent time in two Baltimore City middle schools, observing arts-integrated lessons and speaking to students, teachers, and arts coordinators. The designers realized that in order to understand arts integration, people need to see it in action. The team's solution was a lesson for middle schoolers that taught principles of art and design by engaging the students in making a light-writing video. The resulting video served as a promotional tool for Arts Every Day. The video captured the essence of the organization's message—to actively demonstrate the potential of arts integration in the classroom. The video also incorporated the project's key messages: to put the student at the center, to learn in a tangible and physical way, and to combine two or more subjects to create something new.

Video Creation (below). These stills are from the light-writing lesson and sixty-second promotional video. See the whole video at danube.mica.edu/cdp.

Light Writing (opposite). Here, the students practice writing symbols with flashlights. Design: Julie Diewald, Michael Milano, Aaron Talbot.

LEARNING

EDUCATING

TEACHING

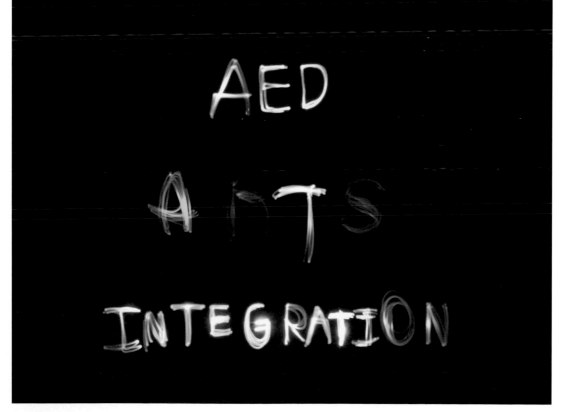

AED

ARTS

INTEGRATION

02

all i want
TO DO
is write
THINGS
down for
YOU

"Sometimes an idea can be our worst enemy, especially if it blocks our thinking of alternatives."

Don Koberg and Jim Bagnall

How to Get Ideas

Once you have defined your problem, it's time to devise solutions and develop concepts in greater depth. This often means communicating ideas to yourself and to other designers on your team as well as to clients and potential end users. An intriguing sketch from your notebook or a provocative phrase scribbled on a whiteboard can now become a concept with a concrete shape and a vivid story to tell.

The first phase of the design process involves casting a wide net around your problem; along the way, you may come up with dozens of different concepts, from the obvious to the outlandish. Before devoting time and energy to developing a single solution, designers open their minds to numerous possibilities and then zero in on a few. The tools explored in this chapter include ways to generate variations on a single concept as well as ways to quickly explore, explain, and expand on a core idea.

With a single-frame project like a book cover, poster, or editorial illustration, the move from ideation to execution is fluid and direct. With complex projects such as websites, publications, and motion graphics, designers tend to work schematically using diagrams, storyboards, and sequential presentations before developing the visual details and appearance of a solution. Physical and digital mock-ups help designers and clients envision a solution in use.

Visual Brain Dumping

Traditional brainstorming is a verbal activity that is often performed in groups. The technique shown here transforms brainstorming into a visual medium better suited for working individually.

Designer Luba Lukova is known worldwide for creating hard-hitting posters that revolve around a single strong image. In many of her pieces, two ideas converge to create an arresting visual statement. This collision of concepts creates a third meaning that is more powerful than the sum of its parts. The resulting posters simmer with humor and conflict.

Lukova's design process begins with intensive sketching. After defining the emotional or political content she wants to convey, she creates dozens of small drawings. For a poster for a performance of *The Taming of the Shrew*, Lukova sought out surprising ways to depict the age-old theme of the battle of the sexes. Her initial ideas included a bra made of two faces and a heart squeezed in a vise. Several sketches show a woman wearing a horse's bridle; the final image compresses the idea further by equipping the woman with a muzzle shaped like a man. *Ellen Lupton and Jennifer Cole Phillips*

"I keep an archive of good sketches that have not been used because they can often trigger an idea for another project."

Luba Lukova

The Taming of the Shrew. Sketches and poster for the Center for Theater Studies at Columbia University. Design: Luba Lukova.

How to Make a Visual Brain Dump

01 **Start sketching.** After defining the basic purpose and parameters of your project, get some paper and a pencil and start making quick, small drawings.

02 **Set a time limit.** In a twenty-minute period, shoot for at least twenty sketches. Put many small drawings on each page so that you can compare them.

03 **Keep moving.** Rather than erasing and refining one sketch, make alternative views of the same idea. Review your ideas and choose some to pursue further.

A LECTURE BY MAUREEN DOWD
92ND STREET Y, NYC THURSDAY, OCT 30, 2010 9:00PM WWW.92ND.ORG

BLUE IS THE
NEW BLACK
WHAT'S MAKING WOMEN SAD?

Blue Is the New Black. The designer was asked to create a poster for a lecture about why contemporary women report being unhappy despite all the apparent economic and social gains they have achieved over the past several generations. She made dozens of quick sketches about the lecture's theme before developing concepts visually. Design: Kimberly Gim.

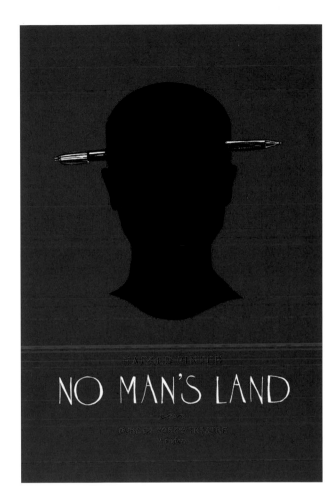

HAROLD PINTER

NO MAN'S LAND

DUKE OF YORK'S THEATRE
LONDON

No Man's Land. In a workshop led by Lukova, designers developed sketches and finished posters for a production of *No Man's Land*, a brooding existential play about some drunken and confused literary types spending a long and terrible night together. Design: Virginia Sasser.

Case Study
Psychological States

In addition to sketching with pen and paper, designers collect images to build databases of visual ideas. Here, designers were asked to create a word mark describing a psychological state. Instead of making word lists or thumbnail sketches, designers compiled databases of images capturing the tenor of their subject. They looked for images drawn from their own personal associations with their word. Just as verbal brainstorming requires moving beyond the obvious to get to fresh ground, visual brainstorming urges participants to find deeper or less obvious responses and associations. The word-mark solutions are a natural outgrowth of this visual search.

Anxious. Itchy, rushed, self-absorbed, solicitous, and spooked: this study digs deep beneath the surface. Design: Katy Mitchell.

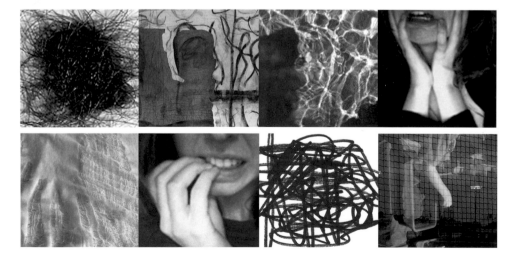

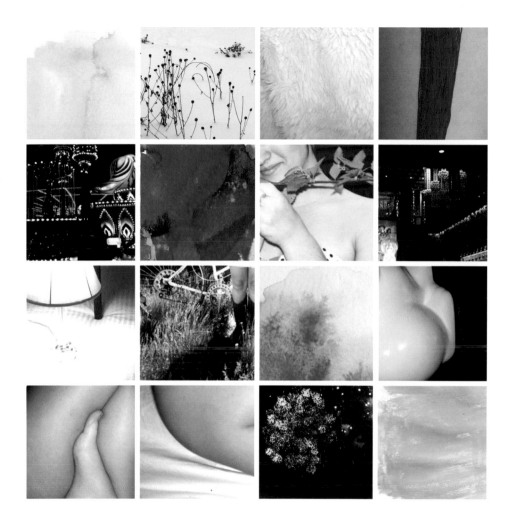

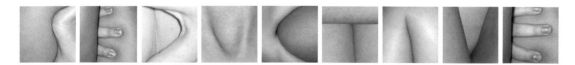

Seductive. Soft, silky, sparkling, hot, red, concealed,
and revealed: this database of images mines the senses.
Design: Heda Hokshirr.

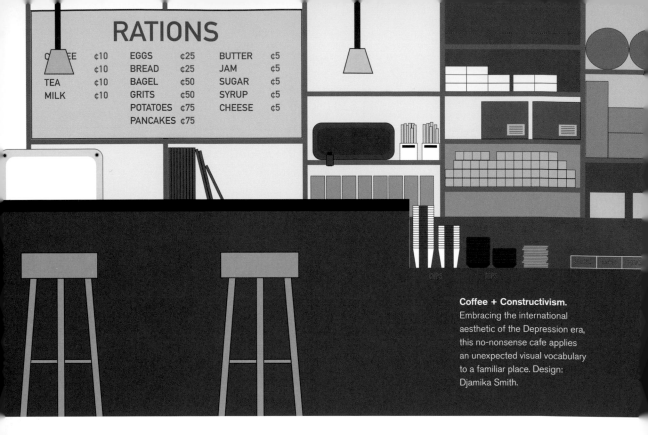

RATIONS

COFFEE	¢10	EGGS	¢25	BUTTER	¢5
	¢10	BREAD	¢25	JAM	¢5
TEA	¢10	BAGEL	¢50	SUGAR	¢5
MILK	¢10	GRITS	¢50	SYRUP	¢5
		POTATOES	¢75	CHEESE	¢5
		PANCAKES	¢75		

Coffee + Constructivism. Embracing the international aesthetic of the Depression era, this no-nonsense cafe applies an unexpected visual vocabulary to a familiar place. Design: Djamika Smith.

Forced Connections

From cookie dough ice cream to zombie/Jane Austen novels, intriguing ideas often result when unlikely players collide. By brainstorming lists of products, services, or styles, and then drawing links between them, designers can forge concepts imbued with fresh wit and new functions. For example, most java houses today look alike. They feature dark reds and browns, wooden tables and floors, and—if you're lucky—a comfortable couch. But what if a cafe had constructivist decor instead? Or what if your errand to the print shop doubled as your coffee break? Likewise, laundromats get a rap for being dirty and dingy, yet public laundries offer a greener alternative to individually owned appliances. How could you make a trip to the laundromat a more inviting experience? Combining services or applying unexpected styles can change the way we think about predictable categories. *Lauren P. Adams and Beth Taylor*

Don Koberg and Jim Bagnall discuss the idea of forced connections as a tool for product designers in their book *The Universal Traveler: A Soft-Systems Guide to Creativity, Problem-Solving, and the Process of Reaching Goals* (San Francisco: William Kaufmann, 1972).

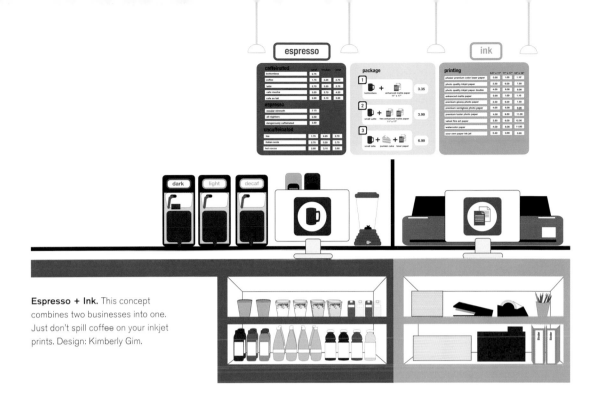

Espresso + Ink. This concept combines two businesses into one. Just don't spill coffee on your inkjet prints. Design: Kimberly Gim.

How to Force a Connection

01 Choose a connection. Depending on whether you are designing a business service, a logotype, or a piece of furniture, decide what kinds of connections to force. Maybe you want to combine services (gym + laundromat), aesthetics (serious literature + cheap horror), or functions (sofa + work space).

02 Make two lists. Let's say your goal is to design a new kind of coffee shop. Brainstorm lists of functions—tailor, pet grooming,

bicycle repair. Make connections and imagine the results. What would each new business be called? What needs does it address? Who is the audience? Would you want to go there?

03 Combine styles, messages, or functions. Identify conflicting or overlapping ideas embodied in your core problem (museum + nature, school + lunch, coffee + economy). Create lists of images and ideas associated with each element, and draw connections between them.

04 Choose one or more viable ideas. Make simple graphic images of interiors, products, and other applications to bring your concept to life. Your choices of forms, color, language, and typography can all speak to the core conflicts embodied in your concept. Use your forced connections to uncover the aesthetic and functional possibilities of your idea. Flat, graphic diagrams like the ones shown above quickly flesh out the main features of an idea without getting burdened with specifics.

Case Study
Laundromats

These visual proposals for new laundromats resulted from the process of forced connections. Designers Beth Taylor and Lauren P. Adams developed ideas by looking at different styles and functions that could transform a laundromat from a dreary place to a pleasant destination.

Agitate + Percolate. This concept applies retro graphics to a combined laundromat/coffee shop. The designer created photomontages and product illustrations to visualize the concept. The logo reflects the company's nostalgic attitude, while the apron-style uniform emphasizes the fun part of the experience: enjoying coffee while your laundry spins and dries. Design: Beth Taylor.

Laundromat + Gym (top). Maximize your time by working out while your clothes wash—and enjoy the sauna while they tumble dry. Design: Beth Taylor.

Laundromat + 50s Mod (bottom). Chit-chat with friends in a retro setting. Designers can use simple drawings to suggest interior spaces. Design: Lauren P. Adams.

Case Study
Multipurpose Tools

Your house is filled with tools. What happens when you combine two or more of these instruments to make something new? This quick exercise using forced connections yields some ideas that are impractical or absurd but others that could become real products with clever functions. Designer Lauren P. Adams started with verbal lists and then made sketches combining ideas from different lists.

Office Tools	Kitchen Tools	Garage Tools
thumbtack	spatula	wrench
stapler	ladle	hammer
scissors	whisk	nail
masking tape	knife	tape measure
hole puncher	tongs	T-square
pencil	vegetable peeler	trowel
glue	corkscrew	handsaw
ruler	can opener	clamp
marker	drink shaker	screw
compass	measuring cup	screwdriver
paperclip	dish scrubber	level
staple remover	grater	staple gun
	funnel	sledgehammer
	rolling pin	
	sieve	

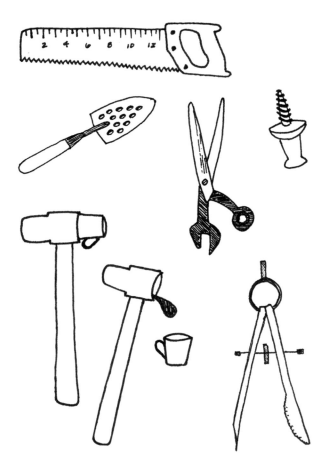

Handsaw + Ruler. Nearly every saw cut requires measuring first, so why not add a ruler to the saw blade?

Grater + Trowel. Scoop up your freshly grated cheese, or crumble chunks of hardened dirt before planting.

Scissors + Wrench. This looks like a clever idea until you consider trying to actually cut something.

Thumbtack + Screw. The thumbtack head would give your hand something to grip while the screw threads make a secure connection.

Sledgehammer + Drink Shaker. The motion of hammering is similar to the motion used to shake a drink. (Sober up before swinging that hammer around.)

Compass + Knife. Cut your cookies to an exact dimension with this gadget for the cook who loves math.

Case Study
Visual Puns

Designers often use humor to hook the viewer's interest. Slamming disparate elements together yields unexpected offspring, and when the result is awkward enough to be funny, viewers come away with a laugh. Cleverness often carries a critical edge as well. In the visual puns shown here, designer Ryan Shelley created dark imagery out of recognizable brands, inviting the viewer into a Dr. Seuss–like world where cars, phones, and Barbie dolls take on sinister identities.

Quality Control. Iconic products are combined with unpleasant forms (guns, pills, bombs, sharks), creating a commentary on the grimmer side of capitalism. The designer translated these graphic icons into graffiti stencils.

Minify: City Cabin

Magnify: Giant Garage

Rearrange: Sleep In the Kitchen

Reverse: Live in the Garden

Rethinking the House. Koberg and Bagnall used action verbs to think about the house in new ways in *The Universal Traveler* (1972). They got the idea from Alex F. Osborn, who presented this technique in his book *Applied Imagination* (1953). Concepts: Don Koberg and Jim Bagnall. Sketches: Lauren P. Adams.

Action Verbs

Alex F. Osborn, who became famous for inventing brainstorming, devised other useful techniques that encourage creativity. One process involves taking an initial idea and applying different verbs to it, such as magnify, rearrange, alter, adapt, modify, substitute, reverse, and combine. These verbs prompt you to take action by manipulating your core concept. Each verb suggests a structural, visible change or transformation. Designers can use this exercise to quickly create fresh and surprising variations on an initial idea. Even a cliché image such as the grim reaper or hitting the bull's-eye can take a surprising turn when you subject it to actions. Designers can apply this technique to objects and systems as well as images. Try reinventing an everyday object such as a house, a book, or a couch by imagining it in a different scale, material, or context. *Lauren P. Adams*

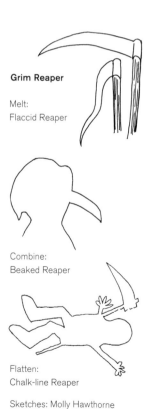

Grim Reaper

Melt:
Flaccid Reaper

Combine:
Beaked Reaper

Flatten:
Chalk-line Reaper

Sketches: Molly Hawthorne

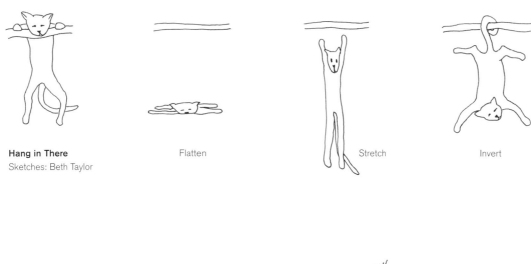

Hang in There
Sketches: Beth Taylor

Flatten

Stretch

Invert

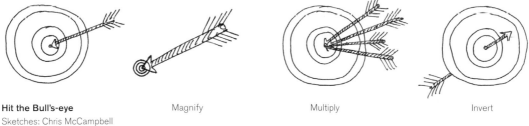

Hit the Bull's-eye
Sketches: Chris McCampbell

Magnify

Multiply

Invert

How to Activate an Idea

01 Start with a basic concept.
Maybe it's an obvious idea, such as using a target to represent performance or a struggling kitten to show courage. Like many clichés, these familiar images provide a common ground for communication.

02 Apply a series of actions to the core image or idea. Create quick sketches. In addition to the words illustrated above, try more unusual ones like melt, dissect, explode, shatter, or squeeze. Don't judge your sketches or spend too much time on one idea; move quickly through your list.

03 Step back and look at what you did. Have you given a new twist to an old cliché? Have you solved a familiar problem in a fresh way? Have you a new ending to an old story? (What if the kitten falls out of the tree? What if the grim reaper kicks his own bucket?) Find your best ideas and take them farther.

swing

play

snack

nap

clean

create

Crayon Daycare Identity. To create this signage system, the designer used action verbs to transform an image of a crayon into different icons. Each one represents an activity station at a daycare center. Design: Lauren P. Adams.

Case Study
Active Icons

In the identity concepts shown here, designers used action verbs to create variations on core ideas. Using a crayon as its basic image, a signage program for a childcare center implements actions such as bend, soften, transform, melt, wring, and frame to depict the familiar crayon in new shapes. Likewise, an icon for a toy store begins with a common image (a puzzle piece), which is transformed in unexpected ways by the application of a series of actions.

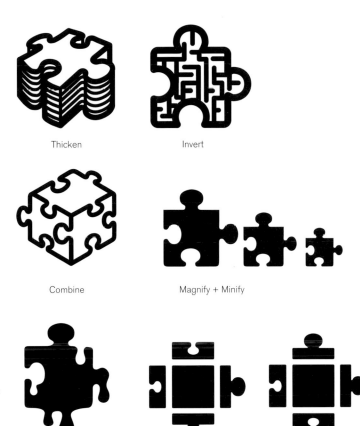

Thicken

Invert

Combine

Magnify + Minify

Puzzle Pieces. Puzzle pieces are a common symbol for toys and for thinking, so they make a good starting point for representing an educational toy store. These sketches and designs put an active spin on an old cliché. Design: Supisa Wattanasansanee.

Melt

Dissect

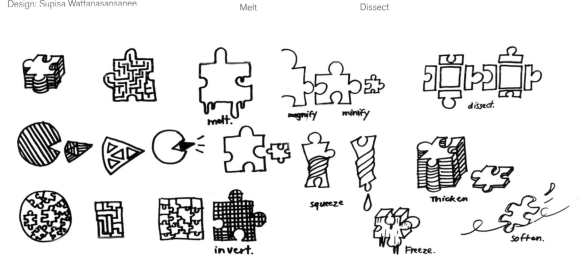

Everything from Everywhere

Graphic designers are barraged by the work of other designers and artists. They are also in constant contact with nature and science, news media and pop culture, high art and visual pollution. Many artists and authors turn inward to encounter sparks of meaning, yet inspiration also comes from the outside world. Instead of churning out work inspired exclusively by client briefs and last year's design annuals, designers should look everywhere for inspiration and ideas.

Systems and grids exist in nature, from the human circulatory system to tree bark and rock formations. Literature offers a bottomless supply of imagery—Dante's hell is a model for circular worlds, and Shakespeare's tropes are an endless source of narrative invention. Designers sometimes fall short of painters and playwrights in looking beyond their own field. Many are comfortable with pillaging scientific graphs for stylistic cues without fully understanding their structure. This resistance to external inspiration is hardly unique to designers; many people refuse to eat new foods or stray far past their TV sets.

By looking beyond the familiar, designers can pull everything from everywhere. Designers can discover ideas for colors, typefaces, illustrations, and texture from the worlds of art, nature, media, and science. Looking everywhere can help designers unlock humor by slamming together disparate elements into new concepts. (*See Forced Connections, page 68.*) Ideas can come from anywhere, but nothing comes from nowhere. All artists draw from the culture around them. *Ryan Shelley and Wesley Stuckey*

Learn to look past your own navel for ideas.

Tectonics. In the poster at right, the designer used wood type to imply colliding plates.

Rock Music. The rhythm and graphics of rock music provide a ideas about color and tactility.

Subway Maps. The gridlike forms of a subway map imply urban life and urban structure.

Texture. The poster's hand-drawn texture is denser at the center, implying the radiating damage of the quake.

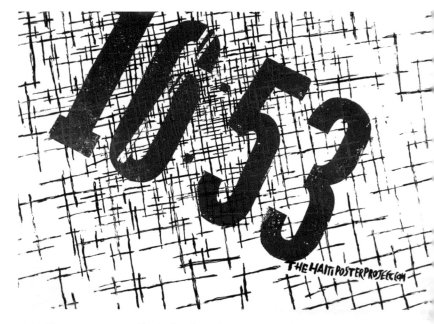

16:53. This poster was created for the Haiti Poster Project, launched after an earthquake struck Haiti at 16:53 PM, January 12, 2010. The Haiti Poster Project invites designers and artists to donate signed, limited-edition posters. The proceeds go toward Doctors Without Borders. The Haiti Poster Project was founded by Leif Steiner and Josh Higgins. Design: Ryan Shelley.

How to Get Everything from Everywhere

01 Be a sponge. Not like a scrub-the-sink sponge, but like a sea sponge. Be actively absorbent, sifting for food. Notice everything. Most importantly, read everything— J. R. R. Tolkien was a genius, and all artists can learn from geniuses.

02 Keep a sketchbook. If your best friend's shirt looks cool against your carpet, note the colors. If song lyrics spark ideas for a photo shoot, write them down. Eventually, this motley assortment of notes will prove invaluable. Many good ideas come in the shower, so having a keen memory helps too.

03 Observe other artists and designers. Learn how they get their ideas, and then try to do the same. Look at everything: there's always something new to learn.

04 Make a database. Collect books, explore songwriting, and visit the zoo. Bookmark images and ideas online. Try building a grid based on dance movements. Making a personal database is like building a library where you can borrow components on demand.

05 Work with a concept in mind. Synthesizing diverse elements is tricky, but framing decisions through a specific form or conceptual idea can help the design process flow smoothly.

Case Study
The Haiti Poster Project

Three designers who donated posters to The Haiti Poster Project documented their source material, showing how a single topic can be interpreted differently based on visual and conceptual cues.

Mandala. These Buddhist markings represent peace, tranquility, and meditation. They also designate sacred spaces.

Line. The continuous line references the links between Haiti, the world relief effort, and the global Haitian diaspora.

Dirt. The rough, red color and texture of the paper mirror the raw grit of the damaged ground.

Map. As in an earthquake map, rings indicate the reach of the event.

Design: Chris McCampbell.

French Toile. Illustrative fabric patterns from French China reference Haiti's French roots and its picturesque coastal views.

Red Cross. The Red Cross symbol represents help, peace, relief, and hope, as well as injury and pain.

Lens. The circle references how the tragedy in Haiti has been seen by foreigners, primarily through the media.

Planet Earth. The circular forms in the poster refer to Haiti as an island on Earth.

Design: Wesley Stuckey.

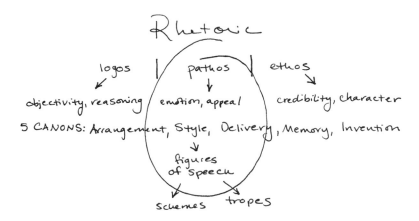

Rhetorical Figures

For centuries, poets, speakers, and writers have used carefully crafted patterns of language to appeal to people's *logos*, *pathos*, and *ethos*, or "reasoning," "emotions," and "ethics." Rhetoric, or the art of communication, forces active connections between concepts. Rhetorical devices not only create a level of seduction, persuasion, and beauty with words, they can do the same for design. According to Aristotle's *Rhetoric* (ca. 350 B.C.E.), the three elements of an effective argument are "first, the means of producing persuasion; second, the style, or language, to be used; third, the proper arrangement of the various parts of the speech." Designers also play with modes of persuasion, style, and arrangement. Of particular value to designers are rhetorical figures, or those literary forms and tactics that deviate from ordinary communication.

Figures of speech enhance meaning while ornamenting the rhythm and sound of language. A *scheme* is a figure of speech that alters the expected word order of a statement or phrase, while a *trope* plays with the meaning of that statement or phrase. Rhetorical figures, while typically referring to verbal language, can also apply to images. These structures can serve as tools for generating concepts or suggesting alternate arrangements. Just as using figures of speech in language helps a writer depart from conventional form, applying them to images, objects, and layouts helps separate a work of design from ordinary practices, making it…well, more poetic. *Virginia Sasser*

Aristotle codified the art of persuasion in *Rhetoric*, ed. W. D. Ross, trans. W. Rhys Roberts (New York: Cosimo Classics, 2010). Hanno Ehses and Ellen Lupton apply rhetorical principles to graphic design in *Design Papers: Rhetorical Handbook* (New York: The Cooper Union, 1988).

Vampire Rhetoric
Synecdoche, metonymy, and antithesis

Basic Figures of Speech

01 Allusion. Reference to a person, place, or thing. *The sidewalk became his own Jackson Pollock.*

02 Amplification. Embellishing an image by listing its particulars. *The snake's rattle—its scaly, beige, ominous rattle—warned me to halt.*

03 Anastrophe. Reversal of normal word order. *Into the pristine lake the plump boy cannonballed.*

04 Anthimeria. Replacing one part of speech for another, such as a verb or an adjective for a noun. *Unhand me, you beast!*

05 Antithesis. Presenting opposite ideas in a parallel form. *Not that I loved dogs more, but I loved cats less.*

06 Ellipsis. Omitting elements that are implied by the context. *I love my dog; and he, the frisbee.*

07 Hyperbole. Rhetorical exaggeration for the purpose of emphasis or humor. *You could see her hesitation from outer space.*

08 Litotes. A form of understatement, often using double negatives. *Her personality was not unlike sandpaper.*

09 Metaphor. Comparing unlike things or ideas to demonstrate their shared qualities. *Her friend the vampire is a hungry mosquito in summertime.*

10 Metonymy. Referencing a term by naming something that is commonly attributed to it. *The pen is mightier than the light saber.*

11 Paradox. Contradictory statement or ironic absurdity that goes against intuition. *I'm too old for gray hair.*

12 Paronomasia. Pun or wordplay utilizing similar sounding words. *These nachos are not yours.*

13 Personification. Attributing human qualities to inanimate objects or abstract ideas. *The moon grinned and winked at the stealthy yeti.*

14 Polyptoton. Repetition of words drawn from the same root. *I didn't follow the leader; I led him right into the coup.*

15 Repetition. The repetition of a word or phrase within a larger clause. *I bake to eat; I bake to feed; I bake to procrastinate.*

16 Synecdoche. Using a part of an object to represent its whole. *He only dated her because he dug her wheels.*

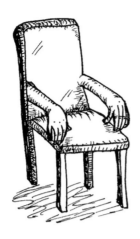

Personification. Human qualities are attributed to the chair.

Metonymy. *Throne* is a word commonly used to refer to a king or ruler.

Allusion. The pipe alludes to Sigmund Freud.

Case Study
Rhetorical Chairs

Writers employ figures of speech to express ideas through a nonstandard use of language; designers can implement these same techniques to make unexpected use of both images and words. In writing, figures of speech often express ideas by evoking a mental picture. Such images help readers remember the message by casting a new light on familiar elements. Here, designer Virginia Sasser has created a series of chairs to demonstrate rhetorical figures. An exercise like this prompts designers to think conceptually about a problem instead of going straight for the literal answer. (No paronomasia intended.)

Anastrophe. Mounting legs to the seat inverts the natural order of the chair.

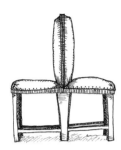

Antithesis. The chairs are similar in structure but face opposite directions.

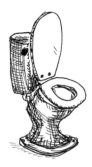

Anthimeria. The toilet seat is repurposed for use as a chair.

Ellipsis. One of the chair legs is left out of the picture.

Hyperbole. The extra-tall office chair exaggerates its adjustability.

Litotes. A cushion on the floor under-states the chair's purpose.

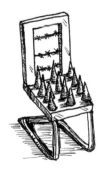

Paradox. Spikes undermine the conventional use of a chair.

Repetition. The legs mirror the pattern of holes on the chair back.

Synecdoche. A whole office chair is implied from just a wheeled base.

Experience Acela. In this series of advertising illustrations, the train becomes a visual metaphor, depicting various attributes of train travel. The images omit the physical seating (ellipsis). The laid-back postures of the passengers serve as metonymies for the train's loungelike furniture. The result is a provocative depiction of the ease and pleasure of rail travel. Illustration: Christoph Niemann. Art director: Megan McCutcheon. Agency: Arnold Worldwide. Client: Amtrak.

No Man's Land. Empty chairs stand in for the two main characters (metonymy). The contrasting styles of chair suggest the opposing emotions of the characters (personification). Poster created in a workshop taught by Luba Lukova. Design: Ann Liu.

One World Flags. The three designs shown opposite were created for a competition sponsored by *Adbusters* magazine. The challenge was to create a flag representing "one world."

Icon, Index, Symbol

Semiotics (also called semiology) is the study of how signs work. Semiotics was conceived at the turn of the twentieth century as an analytical tool for use by linguists, anthropologists, and cultural critics. It has fueled a variety of intellectual traditions, from pragmatist philosophy and structural anthropology to poststructuralist criticism in literature and art.

Designers can use semiotics to generate meaningful forms as well as to study existing signs and communications. For example, when creating a logo or a system of icons, designers can look at the basic categories of visual signs in order to generate ideas with various degrees of abstraction or familiarity.

The American philosopher Charles S. Peirce and his follower Charles Morris identified three basic types of sign: icon, index, and symbol. An icon (such as a drawing of a tree) bears a physical resemblance to the idea it represents. An index points to its referent or is a trace or direct impression of an object or event. A shadow of a tree or a fruit or seed that has fallen to the ground is an index of the tree. Indexical signs often signal a physical action or process. Smoke indicates fire; symptoms indicate disease; an arrow highlights a given direction. Finally, a symbol is abstract (such as the written word *tree*); its form bears no resemblance to its meaning.

Visual signs often embody attributes of more than one sign category. A bathroom sign showing a woman in a dress is an icon (depicting the human figure), but it is also an index (pointing to a toilet facility). *Supisa Wattanasansanee*

Charles S. Peirce founded semiotics in the late nineteenth century. See *Philosophical Writings of Peirce*, ed. Justus Buchler (New York: Dover, 1955). For a visual introduction to semiotics, see Sean Hall, *This Means This, This Means That: A User's Guide to Semiotics* (London: Laurence King, 2007).

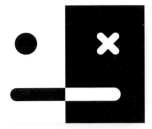

One World Icon. This solution approaches the problem pictorially, creating a divided face that represents the universal experiences of life and death. Although the face is a recognizable icon, the decision to represent death (and a closed eye) with an *x* is symbolic. Design: Justin Kropp.

One World Index. In place of a static mark, this design suggests an open situation. A fill-in-the-blank form can be completed by any person in countless ways. The *x* marking a place to sign and the blank line are indexical signs that trigger an action. Design: Molly Hawthorne.

One World Symbol. Here, the numeral one enclosed inside a circle represents world unity through an abstract symbol and a geometric shape. The circle is not purely abstract, however—it has an iconic relationship to the Earth. Design: Aaron Walser.

Icon. A drawing of a dog's body or face resembles a dog.

Index. The bark of a dog or the tinkle of its collar indicate the creature's physical presence.

Symbol. The word *dog* is an abstraction that does not look or sound like a dog.

Three Kinds of Sign

01 Icon. An icon uses shape, color, sound, texture, and other graphic elements to create a recognizable connection between image and idea. Although icons appear to be naturally linked to their referents, icons rely on cultural convention to varying degrees.

02 Index. An index points to its object rather than representing it abstractly or pictorially. Dog bones, dog dishes, and dog houses are familiar objects that can stand in place of the dog itself. Indexical signs often present designers with the most intriguing solutions.

03 Symbol. A symbol is abstract. The most common symbols we use are words. The alphabet is another set of symbols, designed to represent the sounds of language. The letters *d*, *o*, and *g* have an arbitrary relationship to the sounds they depict.

Case Study
Buddha Herbal Foundation of Thailand

Buddhist-Thai Herbs is a company bearing the seal of Thai Royal Patronage. Designer Supisa Wattanasansanee, working for Cadson Demak Co., Ltd., chose to represent the company with a lotus, which is a famous Thai herb as well as the primary flower of the Buddhist religion. In her sketches and design studies, she created decorative abstractions (symbols) of the lotus form as well as naturalistic images (icons). The final mark references several ideas at once—and several different types of sign. At first glance, it resembles a lotus flower and thus functions as an icon. Simultaneously, its negative shapes resemble a tree and a leaf (combining icon and index). The positive form also approximates a meditating figure, offering another level of iconography as well as a symbol of Buddhism. The resulting graphic image is a compact, visually simple sign that conveys multiple layers of meaning.

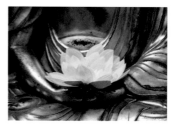

Buddha image © Fred de Noyelle/Godong/Corbis. Lotus image © Paulo Ferreira/istockphoto.

Collaboration

Have you ever seen a collaborative design project fall on its face? (From a thirty-story drop. Onto poison spikes.) Sometimes, designers let their individuality get in the way of teamwork. Effective collaboration yields something new, not a Frankensteinian mash up of parts. In a productive team, each member has ownership over some aspect of the project, bringing a valuable set of perspectives and skills to the group, but each person is willing to merge individual ideas into the bigger structure. The aphorism "two brains are better than one" does not apply to two brains crammed inside one skull. Networks aren't ten hard drives thrown into one box, but rather ten different components that share and communicate.

Working together often involves an element of play. Humor, intelligence, and experimentation are integral to crafting engaging ideas. Sometimes, the best ideas evolve from conversations. Designers pride themselves on interacting with their clients, but designers also need to communicate well with each other. A satisfying collaboration is like building a superfort out of Legos with your friends when everyone shares the bricks. The result will be different from what any one person expected. *Ryan Shelley and Wesley Stuckey*

"The space between people working together is filled with conflict, friction, strife, exhilaration, delight, and vast creative potential."

Bruce Mau

Reinvent **Mural.** These icons for a public mural were designed collaboratively. Design: Lauren P. Adams, Christina Beard, Chris McCampbell. Curator: Cathy Byrd, Maryland Art Place.

How to Collaborate

01 Sit together. Work at the same table so that ideas can develop in relation to each other. Skype and iChat don't count.

02 Hear and be heard. Nobody has the same experience and background as you; other team members are counting on your eye to help mold a unique outcome. Collaboration involves listening as well as talking, giving as well as taking. A degree of conflict is inevitable in any project—learn to go with the flow.

03 Identify leaders. Leadership can be both formal and informal. In corporate settings, groups tend to have an assigned leader. In the looser context of an activist collective or a student collaboration, leadership may emerge organically. Leaders help keep a project on track by distributing duties, representing the team, and prompting decisions when the process stalls. A large team may have several leaders; in a group of just two or three people, everyone could be a leader.

04 Play. But play nice. Everyone's goal should be the overall success of the project, regardless of who initiates various ideas along the way. Just like in a game, a little conflict and competition among players can be good for the process, but don't get stuck on protecting your own contribution. Focus on how a team can achieve more ambitious results than an individual working alone.

Case Study
Reinvent Mural

Maryland Art Place (MAP), an exhibition space in downtown Baltimore, commissioned a mural to enliven the long entrance hall connecting the street to its galleries. The result is *Reinvent*, a continuous sequence of morphing images that depict movement, communication, and the creative process as visitors walk down the hallway. The scale of the project required collaboration. Designers Christina Beard, Lauren P. Adams, and Chris McCampbell developed the initial concept and then implemented the idea, dividing up design and production tasks. The collaborative process hit occasional bumps, but none of the designers could have produced the work single-handedly.

One Thing Leads to Another. The team developed dozens of sequences in which one thing transforms into something else (such as plane/paper airplane/newspaper) and edited them together into a coherent sequence. The final mural consists of over fifty icons spanning a seventy-five-foot wall. At first, the designers had trouble agreeing on a visual strategy. They explored many rendering styles, including photography, flat icons, and 3-D installations. In the end, they were able to combine all of these elements.

Sharing the Load. The team divided up the design of the icons but created guidelines that would unify the project. To integrate the piece with the building's interior, they applied a typographic pattern to the sides of the square columns protruding from the wall and incorporated functional objects, such as a fire alarm, into the graphics. The last transformation in the mural is an exploded 3-D circuit board that suggests how an idea grows and develops.

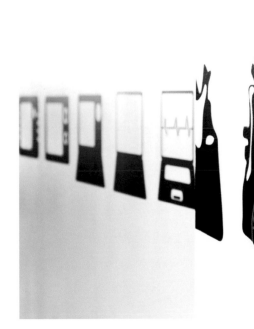

On the principles of co-design, see Elizabeth B. -N. Sanders, "Postdesign and Participatory Culture," 1999, and "Generative Tools for Co-Designing," 2000. http://www.maketools.com/papers-3.html, accessed July 28, 2010.

Co-design

Co-design, or co-creation, is a form of design research that engages end users in the process of building a product, platform, publication, or environment. Designers today have learned that users are experts in their own domains. Many designers now view themselves not as controlling an end result but as putting a process into play that actively involves an audience. Co-creation speaks to the rise of do-it-yourself design culture and an empowered consumer base that seeks to use existing products for new purposes.

Whereas interviews (*see page 26*) and focus groups (*see page 30*) usually serve to define problems and evaluate results, co-design is a generative technique that involves users and audiences in the creative act of making. Co-design emphasizes user experience as design's ultimate result rather than emphasizing the physical features of an object, website, or other design outcome. Experience is where people find value in goods and services. Given the right tools, nondesigners are well-equipped to envision experiences that will satisfy their needs and desires.

How does it work? In the methodology developed by co-design pioneer Elizabeth B. -N. Sanders, a design team provides a group of potential users with a kit of materials that prompts them to imagine their own solutions to a problem. Whether exploring a car, a phone, a software service, or a hospital room, the co-design process often involves graphic communication. Co-design kits typically include a printed background and a set of materials such as images of generic controls, cut-paper elements, photographs, and tools for making drawings, maps, and collages. These kits often frame open-ended questions, such as what will your school look like in the future? The design team looks for insights and ideas that tap the emotional expectations of users. *Ellen Lupton*

"The new rules call for new tools. People want to express themselves and to participate directly and proactively in the design development process."

Elizabeth B. -N. Sanders

Título de sua inscrição

Esboço de suas idéias

Como ele é!
O que ele faz!
Como você vai usar ele!
Quando e onde você vai usar ele!

PAZ

WELCOME
TO IRAC

☐ Para minha identidade
Como este celular mostra sua identidade, i.e., seu gosto, estilo, personalidade, profissão, religião, ou cultura?

☑ Para minha vizinhança
Como este celular melhora a vida na sua vizinhança ou a convivência com seus vizinhos?

Nokia Open Studios. In the developing world, the adoption of mobile technologies is outpacing that of hard-wired computer and phone systems. Designers from Nokia worked with communities living in informal settlements in Brazil, Ghana, and India. Two hundred twenty co-designers envisioned "dream devices." The participant shown here, a hip-hop dance teacher living in Favela do Jacarezinho in Rio de Janeiro, Brazil, pictured a phone that would diminish violence in her community. Nokia design team: Younghee Jung, Jan Chipchase, Indri Tulusan, Fumiko Ichikawa, and Tiel Attar.

How to Co-design

01 Identify co-designers to collaborate with. If you are creating a product for children, work with kids, teachers, and parents. If you are designing a healthcare solution, work with patients and caregivers. Some researchers suggest collaborating with extreme users: for example, work with people with disabilities (who experience barriers to product use) as well as experts (such as fans, collectors, or repair technicians).

02 Define a question. Your research question should be both concrete and open-ended. Don't predetermine the solution. Instead of asking participants to design a better countertop kitchen mixer, ask them to imagine an ideal kitchen environment.

03 Create a co-design kit. Provide simple tools that invite participants of all skill levels to engage actively and freely.

A co-design kit might include a variety of blank and printed stickers or set of inspiring words or questions. Sessions can be planned for either individual or group participation.

04 Listen and interpret. Observe how co-designers engage in the process, and study the results of their work. Don't expect picture-perfect products. Instead, learn from people's hopes, desires, and fears.

Case Study
Design to Empower

One benefit of co-design is the creative experience itself. Designer Giselle Lewis-Archibald conducted a series of workshops with girls living at the Good Shepherd Center, a residential facility in Baltimore for young women experiencing emotional and behavioral difficulties. A workbook prompted the girls to express their influences, ideals, and hopes for the future. Exercises included drawing stickers featuring inspirational words and making a self-portrait from a hand tracing. These exercises culminated with each girl making a simple zine about herself.

Design: Kate

Slips of Fortune

Supplies
- 0.75" x 3.75" slips of paper (above)
- Pens and markers

Directions
- Write notes of advice to your friends.

Design: Giselle Lewis-Archibald

Design: Sierra

Case Study
Graffimi

User-generated content on the Internet is another form of co-design. Graffimi is a virtual graffiti platform that supplies users with tools such as virtual spray paint, brushes, and stencils. Users add their work to a live broadcasting wall that serves as a public canvas. This brick wall, which forms the background of the website, expands as it is filled with submissions from users. Designer Baris Siniksaran created the digital arena; users supply the content that brings it to life.

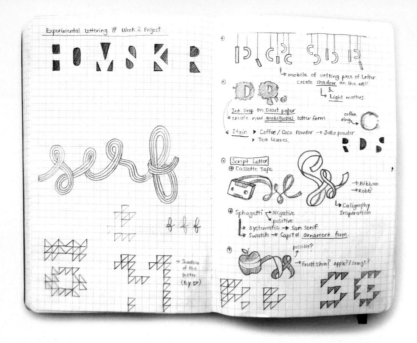

Sketches: Supisa Wattanasansanee

Visual Diary

There's only one salvation from the grind of a never-ending project: break your routine and make something pretty. Designing something new every day can be as healthy for the creative mind as eating fruits and vegetables is for the body. Drawn-out projects stuffed with endless phases, revisions, and brainstorming sessions can rapidly degrade into over-cooked solutions and aimless theory. Sometimes, a big spoonful of sweet, unrefined creation can be the perfect remedy for opening up a stubborn mental block. By making beautiful things on a daily basis, you can build a library of small and simple ideas that can blossom into ambitious projects later. Making something gorgeous can be painless and fulfilling. Hydrate your mind with small pleasures reminiscent of the doodles and sketchbook pages that first got you excited about graphic design. *Christopher Clark*

Do it every day.

A Month of Type. Making a new typographic work each day for a month is a workout for the eye and mind. Design: Christopher Clark.

How to Start a Visual Diary

01 Define parameters. How regular are the entries? Will you work in a journal or post online? Will there be a theme to your diary or will it roam untamed? Ask yourself questions. Experiment with new media and shelved ideas.

02 Stick to the rules. Big projects tend to dominate your schedule. Free yourself by dedicating a little time each day to making something. Fifteen minutes of unguided creativity could solve a month's worth of overthinking.

03 Work in a series. If a certain medium or method excites you, try it again the next day and the next. Make each entry a thoughtful follow-up to the last. That's how little things grow into bigger projects.

04 Share your work. Create a blog or Flickr account. Sign up for an exhibition at a coffee shop. Get friends and coworkers to join in on the noodling. Be inspired by the weight of an audience's gaze. (Of course, you don't have to show everything you make.)

05 Keep going. The more stuff you make, the more valuable the endeavor becomes. Build up a graphic arsenal. When the really tough problems declare war on your sanity, you will be prepared to defend yourself.

06 Harvest the good stuff. Glance through your journal when it's time to tackle bigger projects. You may have already found a useful solution or a viable idea.

Exploring the Everyday. Working with a different typeface every day encourages sampling a variety of styles and media. Designer Christopher Clark started a blog in order to invent an audience. Eventually, a fictional audience became a real one. Starting with phrases he had scribbled in notebooks or saved on his cell phone, he created quick typographic studies.

Values
Change

Lost in Translation

When faced with the task of designing a brand that works in multiple languages, designers often run into conflicting connotations or lost layers of meaning. Cross-cultural naming and branding is not an easy feat. The designers at Toormix develop most of their branding and design work with three languages in mind: Spanish, Catalan, and English. They tackle variations in language by researching and testing the phrases that will appear in their work. This research is integral to their design process. Determining the name of a company or the primary text of a campaign is crucial to the success of any visual solution, and even more so for a cross-cultural audience. Toormix's strategies include steering away from colloquial phrases, avoiding raunchy language, and being wary of phrases imbued with strong cultural associations, which can easily get lost in translation. *Isabel Uria*

"La dificultad del trabajo con tres idiomas con las características de este concepto está en saber ligar las frases."

Ferran Mitjans

Laus 08: FAD (Foment de les Arts i el Disseny). This campaign is for Graphic Pride Day, part of a design festival in Laus, Spain. Design: Ferran Mitjans and Oriol Armengou, Toormix.

How to Not Get Lost in Translation

01 Identify the languages and locales where your project or brand will circulate. Will your project address a multilingual population that lives in the same region, or will it need to function in different parts of the world? Toormix used three languages in their posters for the Laus 08 design festival: Spanish, Catalan, and English.

02 Begin with the language most familiar to you. If you are a native English speaker, start with English. Don't rely on slang, colloquial expressions, and rhyming phrases, which may translate poorly.

03 Research translations. Use a dictionary, but always test your phrases with native speakers.

04 Where possible, use words or symbols that are shared between languages. In the poster above, the words *disseny*, *deseño*, and *design* have a common root and a similar meaning across the three languages. Toormix used the place name Laus and the year 2008 as universal elements that don't require translation.

Case Study
Dollar Store Museum

In a workshop led by Toormix at MICA, designers were asked to create a basic logotype, tag line, and branding concept for a museum of low-cost everyday products. The brand had to make sense when translated from English to Spanish. The Toormix team helped evaluate the viability of each solution.

More/Less. The phrase "more or less" translates easily into Spanish (*más y menos*). The symbol 99¢ requires no translation. Design: Ann Liu and Supisa Wattanasansanee.

more / less
museum of 99¢ things

CHEAP
SH*T

A COLLECTION OF THE USELESS
AND MASS PRODUCED.

M**RDA
BARATA

UNA COLECCIÓN DE LO INÚTIL
Y PRODUCIDO EN MASA.

$ MUSEUM. The dollar sign does not translate to Europe's currency. For use in Spain, the clever breaking of *US* and *EU* between the S form would have to be translated to EEUU and UE. Design: Ryan Shelley.

Cheap Sh*t. The Spanish phrase *mierda barata* is more aggressively vulgar than its English equivalent, "cheap shit." Curse words can prove problematic across languages. Design: Wesley Stuckey.

MUS€O
MU$EUM
dollar store culture

Cheapo. In English, this list of fabricated slang words makes an engaging play with language, but the slang phrases don't translate well into Spanish. Design: Elizabeth Anne Herrmann.

MU$EUM. The words *museum* and *museo* accommodate both the dollar and Euro symbols, making this design a successful bilingual, cross-cultural solution. Design: Ryan Shelley.

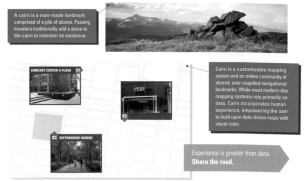

Cairn is a concept for a map-making application that allows users to add landmarks to personalized maps. This simple sequence of slides, developed in a workshop at MICA with Denise Gonzales Crisp, plans out the basic user experience. Design: Jenny Kutnow.

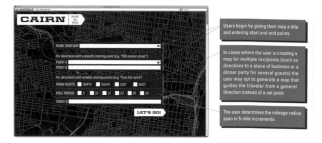

Concept Presentations

Filmmakers, animators, cartoonists, and writers use storyboards to plot out narratives. Graphic designers employ sequential screen-based presentations to develop and explain concepts. This sequential medium is a tool for both thinking and communicating. When creating websites, product concepts, mobile apps, branding campaigns, and other complex projects, designers use schematic sequences to test and communicate ideas in development. Such presentations typically include text as well as visualizations. Digital slides can be projected in a meeting, printed on paper, or distributed online. Designers often submit presentation documents to competitions as well, using the slide format to explain ideas quickly and compactly to a jury. Presentations are an invaluable tool for quickly fleshing out complex concepts. *Ellen Lupton*

For detailed instructions on developing concept presentations, see BJ Fogg, "Conceptual Designs: The Fastest Way to Communicate and Share Your Ideas," in *Design Research: Methods and Perspectives,* ed. Brenda Laurel (Cambridge, MA: MIT Press, 2003), 201–11.

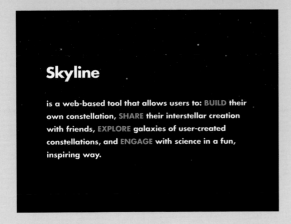

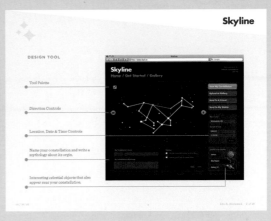

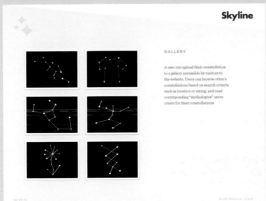

Skyline. This concept proposal shows the basic elements of an app for making custom constellations. Design: Eric Mortensen.

How to Make a Concept Presentation

01 Choose a format. Powerpoint, Keynote, and Adobe PDF formats are easy to email, post online, or print out as well as to project on a screen.

02 Make an outline. Interface designer BJ Fogg suggests setting up a simple template with sections such as title, overview, challenge, prototype views, solution, benefits, and drawbacks.

03 Fill in the blanks. Use your outline as a prompt for quickly fleshing out a concept. Include a header on each page identifying the project, company, or team. Develop details as well as broader views.

04 Keep it simple. Sometimes, imagery that is simple and sketchy helps keep your audience focused on the basic idea rather than on a finished product. Use storyboards and photographs to demonstrate how people will use the product. Make your text concise, direct, and consistent.

Case Study
Online News Services

Interaction designers use schematic screen captures to illustrate product features and narrate typical user interactions before building out functional prototypes. Diagrams and problem statements help designers deliver ideas clearly.

Future Journalism. This proposal describes an online news service that would provide readers with a subscription, granting them access to content from dozens of news agencies. Subscription revenue would be divided among providers according to how much readers use each service. Keeping track of personal news consumption becomes interesting data for users as well. Design: Molly Hawthorne.

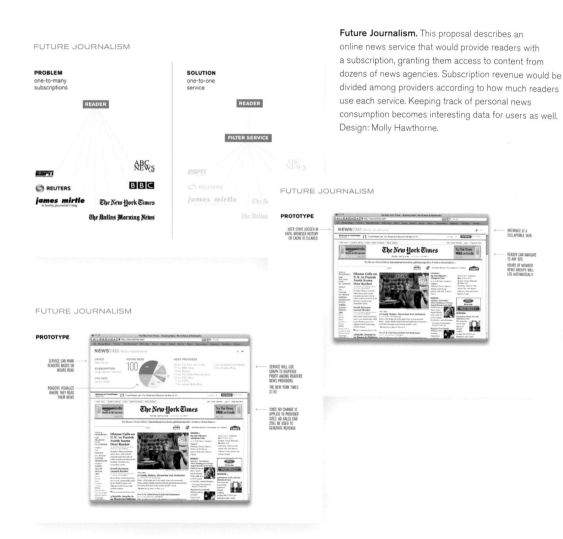

Perks. Service design involves planning how elements will work in a variety of media and situations. This concept presentation describes a new way for news organizations to generate advertising revenue. In the traditional advertising model, pricing is based on a campaign's number of views or impressions. Advertisers today, however, seek measurable responses rather than mere click-counting. The Perks concept would reward readers with coupons from advertisers, creating a direct and positive interaction. The presentation shows how users would join and use the service. Design: Mark Alcasabas.

03

"Learn to detect glimmers of hope
among the debris of failure."

Martin Venezky

How to Create Form

After a period of open-ended research and free thinking, designers hone in on one or more concepts to develop more fully. A wealth of ideas is a great thing, but only a few concepts will make it across the finish line. After selecting the most promising ideas, designers express them visually. As an idea becomes tangible, it comes to life. How does it work? How does it communicate? What does it mean? The answers often send designers back to the initial phases of ideation.

While research and concept development clarify the direction, goals, and underlying ideas that will drive a possible solution, executing the idea remains a crucial task. For many designers, this is the most exciting part of the work and the true test of their abilities. Although some firms focus on defining problems and strategies, leaving implementation to others, most designers are fascinated with how concepts come forward in physical objects, visible images, or usable systems. The most exciting work lies in making it real.

Indeed, some designers see making form as the essence of what they do. Visual invention need not happen at the end of a project. Molding ideas with shapes, colors, surfaces, and materials can precede the conceptual phases that are the traditional foundation of the design process. Concepts can be discovered from the vibrant detritus of open-ended form making.

Preliminary research and analysis comes to naught when concepts are executed in a dull or clumsy fashion. Two designers will interpret a single creative concept in distinctly different ways. Just as deliberate thinking techniques can guide the planning and inception of a project, so too can they inform the processes of visual invention. Conscious methods such as brainstorming and mind mapping can free the mind to discover and invent; likewise, strategies for thinking and making can provide inspiring tools or an open frame of mind that will help designers bring pleasure, delight, and illumination to their work.

ideo shoot http://tweetphoto.com/e7afffb 4:09 PM Oct 14th from web I want to thank my fans for making '3' the # 1 song on the world 3:19 PM Oct 14th from web Britney's new single, '3', debuts at #1 on the Billboard Hot 100! http://bit.ly/1juZAx

Sprinting

Designers sometimes get stuck in routine ways of working: set it flush, add some white space, put a box around it, whatever. When seeking more creative approaches, designers can feel paralyzed by the range of choices and possibilities. Try giving yourself less time to think and more time to act.

Sprinting is a technique for breaking out of your own habits by forcing yourself to come up with a new visual solution in a fixed time frame and then moving on quickly to try something else. Sprinting generates visual directions in short spurts of time. When the time investment is short, designers often feel more comfortable taking risks and trying alternative approaches. Each concept becomes less precious and easier to explore, and then discard. Use a defined set of parameters and a thirty-minute deadline to rein in the process. Schedule your sprints like meetings or calendar events. Be sure to leave gaps between them—each one will leave you exhausted. *Krissi Xenakis*

"Nine-tenths of wisdom is being wise in time."

Theodore Roosevelt

Quick Picks. Lay out your designs on a table and get friends or colleagues to help edit and sort them. Design: Krissi Xenakis.

How to Sprint

01 Set parameters. Define some ground rules, such as a limited range of typefaces and a fixed set of layout elements. You might also create a few sets of rules and rotate them among your sprints.

02 Warm up. Five minutes of speed reading (look at inspiring books) or loose sketching (no computer) will help you get in the mood. Don't count the warm-up in your thirty-minute sprint.

03 Plunge in. Try new ways of working. Ward off brain mush by pacing your sprints throughout the day. Work fast and have fun.

04 Decision time. When you have generated a body of work, print out small versions of your sprints and lay them out like cards on a table. Seeing them all at once makes them easy to sort, compare, and discard. Try sprinting at least four times to get a rich set from which to choose your final piece.

Twitter Typography Series (above). These posters use tweets from the five most heavily subscribed Twitter feeds between October 13 and 15, 2009. In order to experiment with typography in a quick, immediate way, the designer created one hundred posters in a series of thirty-minute design sprints. She chose twenty-five designs to print and display. Design: Krissi Xenakis.

Mars Book Sprints (opposite). The designer employed sprinting in order to generate multiple typographic concepts for a book design. Her parameters included using variations of a centered grid, using only black and white, and using only the typefaces HTF Whitney and Bodoni. The text is from Carl Sagan's *Cosmos* (1980). The designer created a total of twelve page variations. Design: Christina Beard.

WHAT WE DO WITH OUR WORLD,

NUMBERLESS MOMENTS,

HERE WE FACE A CRITICAL BRANCH IN HISTORY,

AND PERHAPS OUR SPECIES AS WELL.

AN
- CARL SAGAN

IMMENSITY OF

SPACE
AND TIME.

OF TIME AND **AN IMMENSITY** AT THIS MOMENT

S

COUNTLESS HERE WE FACE A CRITICAL BRANCH IN HISTORY,

AND OUR SMALL PLANET **WORLDS,**

P

DESTROY OUR CIVILIZATION **NUMBERLESS**

MOMENTS, AND POWERFULLY AFFECT

A

AND PERHAPS OUR SPECIES AS WELL. **WHAT** WITH OUR WORLD,

BRANCH IN HISTORY, **WE DO**

C

WILL PROPAGATE DOWN THROUGH CENTURIES **THE**

DESTINY - CARL SAGAN

OF OUR WELL WITHIN OUR POWER TO

E DECENDANTS,

SPACE

IT IS WELL WITHIN OUR POWER TO DESTROY OUR CIVILIZATION

HERE WE FACE A CRITICAL BRANCH

AND OUR SMALL PLANET

PERHAPS OUR SPECIES AS WELL

WHAT WE DO WITH OUR WORLD,

WILL PROPAGATE DOWN THROUGH CENTURIES AND POWERFULLY AFFECT THE DESTINY OF OUR DECENDANTS,

COUNTLESS WORLDS, NUMBERLESS MOMENTS,

AND TIME.

- CARL SAGAN

---

an immensity of space
countless worlds
is well within our power to destroy our civilization
what we do with our world,
here we face a critical branch in history,
and perhaps our species as well.
numberless moments,
and time.
- carl sagan

Case Study
Newspaper Layout

Newspapers, magazines, and other formatted publications have style guides that serve as ready-made parameters for successful sprinting. Working with given elements such as headlines, decks, photographs, captions, and body text, the designer can focus on arranging the components in a series of quick takes, exploring structured uses of the page grid as well as more relaxed or imaginatively framed solutions. The layouts shown here feature editorial content from *i*, a Portuguese daily newspaper (ionline.pt). The designers used thirty-minute sprints to develop each layout.

"Planespotters." The content for these layouts is a photo essay about people who enjoy watching planes land and take off at airports. Text: Joana Azevedo Viana. Photographs: Dora Nogueira. Design: Katarzyna Komenda and Krissi Xenakis. Editorial content © ionline.pt.

Zoom // Foto-reportagem

Planespotters.
O que eu queria mesmo era ser piloto

Vêm em família, aos fins-de-semana – foi a paixão pelos aviões que os uniu e já contagiaram o seu entusiasmo amais uma geração

Sempre adorei aviões. O meu pai foi piloto da Força Aérea; o meu irmão seguiu-lhe os passos; a minha mãe queria ser astronauta. Toda a minha infância foi passada perto de aviões. Enquanto as outras crianças combinavam jogos de futebol aos fins-de-semana, eu passava os meus no aeródromo de Évora. Ficava horas sentado dentro dos aviões, no cockpit, a sonhar com o dia em que poderia pilotá-los. Aos 17 anos o meu pai ofereceume o brevet licença de condução de aviões) para pilotar planadores. Foi então que descobri que não poderia fazê-los era daltónico. Se não tivesse tido a sorte de nascer no meio dos aviões, estaria hoje ao lado das centenas de planespotters que passam os dias a observar de longe: partilhamos

Tive a sorte de nascer no meio dos aviões e cresci com esta paixão. O dia em que voei pela primeira vez foi simplesmente mágico

esta grande paixão pelos aviões. Como não podia pilotar, tornei-me engenheiro aeronáutico e sócio do meu pai na Agrouar, empresa de aviação que fundou quando voltou da Guiné – depois de a empresa onde trabalhava ter falido e de ter recebido de indemnização um avião. No próximo ano espero concluir o brevet de piloto particular – que recebi como presente de licenciatura. O dia em que voei pela primeira vez a solo foi simplesmentemágico. Ninguém esquece o seu voo de largada. Pilotar envolve muito mais do que adrenalina: é liberdade e responsabilidade, é experimentar um silêncio e uma calma indescritíveis. Nada pode igualar essa sensação. *Rui Dias trata da manutenção dos aviões no aeródromo de Évora*

O ponto de encontro faz-se na estrada para Camarate, que segue ao lado das pistas de aterragem doAeroporto daPortela, em Lisboa. Num dia bom, chegam a conseguir observar as manobras de mais de 50 aviões de diferentes companhias aéreas

São cerca de 500, os spotters portugueses, e muitas vezes a paixão passa de geração em geração. Cada imagem que conseguem é um troféu que exibem com orgulho

De olhos no céu e câmara a postos, o planespotter fotografa cada avião que se aproxima: no bloco de notas ficam registados modelo e companhia aérea, para comparação futura

Por vezes um spotter consegue levar a família, mas este hobbie continua a ser essencialmente masculino

Tempo para gastar e muita paciência fazem um bom spotter

Há quem não se limite a passar um bom bocado. Alguns dos aficionados constroem verdadeiros portfólios que exibem em sites como o da associação portuguesa de entusiastas de aviação (apeapt. com) ou o airliners.net

38 ⓘ —23 Maio 2009

—23 Maio 2009 ⓘ 39

Planespotters.
O que eu queria mesmo era ser piloto

Vêm em família, aos fins-de-semana – foi a paixão pelos aviões que os uniu e já contagiaram o seu entusiasmo amais uma geração
O ponto de encontro faz-se na

Tive a sorte de nascer no meio dos aviões e cresci com esta paixão.
O dia em que voei pela primeira vez foi simplesmente mágico

Sempre adorei aviões. O meu pai foi piloto da Força Aérea, o meu irmão seguiu-lhe os passos, a minha mãe quase se quis ser astronauta. Toda a minha infância foi passada perto de aviões. Enquanto as outras crianças combinavam jogos de futebol aos fins-de-semana, eu passava os meus no aeródromo de Évora. Ficava horas sentado dentro dos aviões, no cockpit, a sonhar com o dia em que poderia pilotá-los. Aos 17 anos o meu pai ofereceu-me a brevê licença de condução de aviões para pilotar planadores. Foi então que descobri que não podería faê-lo era daltónico. Se não tivesse tido a sorte de nascer no meio dos aviões, estaria hoje ao lado das centenas de planespotters que passam os dias a observar de longe, partilhamos esta grande paixão pelos aviões. Como não podia pilotar, tornei-me engen-

heiro aeronáutico e sócio do meu pai na Aegrue, empresa de aviação que fundou quando voltou da Guiné – depois da empresa onde trabalhava ter falido – e ele ter recebido de indemnização um avião. No próximo ano comecei o brevê de piloto particular – que recebi como presente de licenciatura. O dia em que voei pela primeira vez a sós foi simplesmente mágico. Ninguém esquece o seu voo de largada. Pilotar envolve muita adrenalina e liberdade e responsabilidade, é experimentar um silêncio e uma calma indescritíveis. Nada pode igualar essa sensação.

Rui Dias trata da manutenção dos aviões no aeródromo de Évora

1. Tempo para gastar e muita paciência fazem um bom spotter.

2. Vêm em família, aos fins-de-semana – foi a paixão pelos aviões que os uniu e já contagiaram o seu entusiasmo amais uma geração

3. O ponto de encontro faz-se na entrada para Camarate, que segue ao lado das pistas de aterragem doAeroporto daPortela, em Lisboa. Num dia bom, chegam a conseguir observar as manobras de mais de 50 aviões de diferentes companhias aéreas

4. São cerca de 500, os spotters portugueses, e muitas vezes a paixão passa de geração em geração. Cada imagem que conseguem é um troféu que exibem com orgulho

5. De olhos no céu e câmara a postos, o planespotter fotografa cada avião que se aproxima; no bloco de notas ficam registados modelo e companhia aérea, para comparação futura

6. Há quem não se limite a passar um bom bocado. Alguns dos afionados constroem verdadeiros portfólios que exibem em sites como o da associação portuguesa de entusiastas de aviação (apeapt.com) ou o airliners.net

---

Zoom // Foto-reportagem

Sempre adorei aviões. O meu pai foi piloto da Força Aérea, o meu irmão seguiu-lhe os passos, a minha mãe quase se quis ser astronauta. Toda a minha infância foi passada perto de aviões. Enquanto as outras crianças combinavam jogos de futebol aos fins-de-semana, eu passava os meus no aeródromo de Évora. Ficava horas sentado dentro dos aviões, no cockpit, a sonhar com o dia em que poderia pilotá-los. Aos 17 anos o meu pai ofereceu-me a brevê licença de condução de aviões para pilotar planadores. Foi então que descobri que não podería faê-lo era daltónico. Se não tivesse tido a sorte de nascer no meio dos aviões, estaria hoje ao lado das centenas de planespotters que passam os dias a observar de longe, partilhamos esta grande paixão pelos aviões. Como não podia pilotar, tornei-me engenheiro aeronáutico e sócio do meu pai na Aegrue, empresa de aviação que fundou quando voltou da Guiné – depois da empresa onde trabalhava ter falido – e ele ter recebido de indemnização um avião. No próximo ano comecei o brevê de piloto particular – que recebi como presente de licenciatura. O dia em que voei pela primeira vez a sós foi simplesmente mágico. Ninguém esquece o seu voo de largada. Pilotar envolve muita adrenalina e liberdade e responsabilidade, é experimentar um silêncio e uma calma indescritíveis. Nada pode igualar essa sensação.

Rui Dias trata da manutenção dos aviões no aeródromo de Évora

Planespotters.
O que eu queria mesmo era ser piloto

Tive a sorte de nascer no meio dos aviões e cresci com esta paixão.
O dia em que voei pela primei a vez foi simplesmente mágico

Por vezes um spotter consegue levar a família, mas este hobbie continua a ser essencialmente masculino

De olhos no céu e câmara a postos, o planespotter fotografa cada avião que se aproxima; no bloco de notas ficam registados modelo e companhia aérea, para comparação futura

Tempo para gastar e muita paciência fazem um bom spotter.

Vêm em família, aos fins-de-semana – foi a paixão pelos aviões que os uniu e já contagiaram o seu entusiasmo amais uma geração

São cerca de 500, os spotters portugueses, e muitas vezes a paixão passa de geração em geração. Cada imagem que conseguem é um troféu que exibem com orgulho

O ponto de encontro faz-se na entrada para Camarate, que segue ao lado das pistas de aterragem doAeroporto daPortela, em Lisboa. Num dia bom, chegam a conseguir observar as manobras de mais de 50 aviões de diferentes companhias aéreas

Há quem não se limite a passar um bom bocado. Alguns dos afionados constroem verdadeiros portfólios que exibem em sites como o da associação portuguesa de entusiastas de aviação (apeapt.com) ou o airliners.net

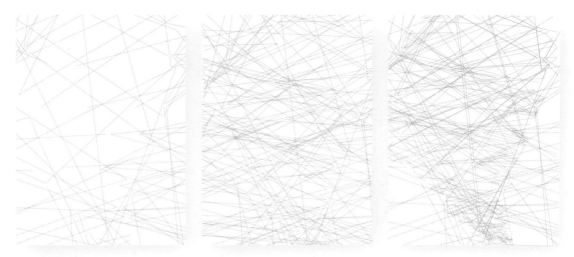

Populating a grid. By laying down a series of lines based on a photo of a tornado shape cut out of paper, the designer created a series of increasingly dense grids. In subsequent iterations, she added grid lines to allow for typography and object placement. Design: Ann Liu.

Alternative Grids

Graphic designers use grids to structure and organize information in newspapers, magazines, and websites. In this book, column grids help create a cohesive look and feel. A single publication might employ different numbers of columns from page to page or screen to screen, but the underlying modules are consistent. Sometimes designers break the grid on purpose, but the grid serves to guide most decisions about scale and placement.

Alternative grids can push the parameters of design to a more experimental realm, enabling designers to explore new ways of arranging content. Designed with different shapes and angles, alternative grids don't follow strict horizontal or vertical lines. They can be developed by looking at everyday objects and images or by creating patterns or textures out of the information being delivered. Rather than focus on efficiency, as would be the case for newspapers, alternative grids serve to explore formal possibilities of layout and typography. *Isabel Uria*

For a collection of pattern-based grids, see Carsten Nicolai, *Grid Index* (Berlin: Die Gestalten Verlag, 2009).

Paper-cut Tornado. Referencing the iconic shape of a tornado, the designer created one out of cut paper, and then photographed it to construct an alternative grid.

Final Poster. Aiming for the illusion of depth, the designer applied gradients to angled lines of type sitting on various grid lines within the tornado. She added the rainbow border as a nod to the technicolor film from *Wizard of Oz*. Design: Ann Liu.

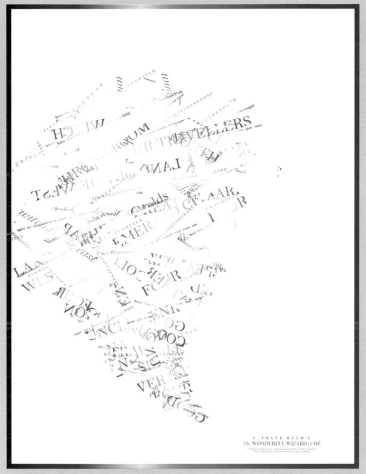

How to Design Alternative Grids

01 Observe. Designers create patterns and grids out of endless sources, including the natural and man-made worlds. Cityscapes, architecture, trees, animals, weather patterns, and rock formations are among the inspirations. Explore the environment around you, or look at works of art and design.

02 Replicate. Take a photograph or make a quick sketch of forms that catch your attention. Later, look for linear structures in the image. To create the experimental poster above, designer Ann Liu sketched a tornado. She then abstracted the sketch into a network of overlapping lines that cover the entire surface of the page.

03 Organize. Begin arranging typography and other elements in response to the underlying pattern of the grid. In addition to using the lines to guide the placement of elements, you can use them to cut, crop, distort, and overlap. The grid becomes a tool for open-ended play rather than rational construction.

Case Study
Amazon Posters

These typographic studies harvest text and data from Amazon.com about specific books. The designers used alternative grids to structure this found information.

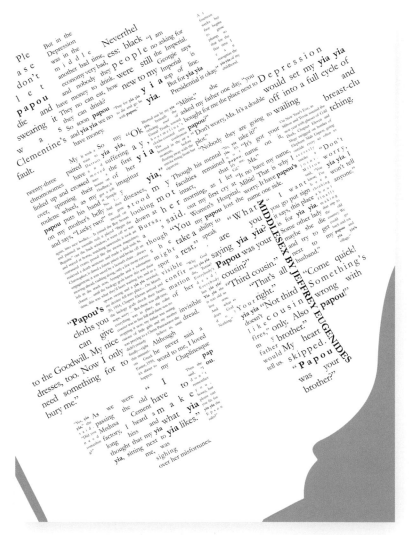

View from the Top. The designer used a street map of the setting to structure text about *Middlesex* (2007), by Jeffrey Eugenides. Design: Krissi Xenakis.

"All visual information and forms, whether illustration, graphic design, painting, or architecture, are comprised of two-dimensional grids and patterns, much like the way that computer information is made up of zeroes and ones." Carsten Nicolai

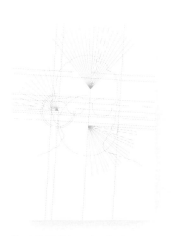

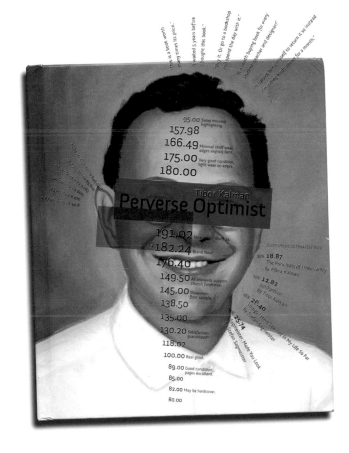

Face Grid. This poster about Tibor Kalman's classic monograph *Perverse Optimist* (2000) uses a grid derived from facial features. Design: Chris McCampbell.

Case Study
Tessellated Grids

A tessellation is a pattern of shapes covering a plane with no overlaps or gaps and appears in traditional tile work and decorative art. The lines in a tessellated pattern can inspire multiple grids.

Folded-paper Tessellation. This complex pleated-paper design uses a geometric grid. Like all of the patterns illustrated on this spread, this pattern is a variation of interlocking triangles. Original folded paper design: Eric Gjerde. Paper folding and photography: Isabel Uria.

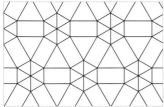
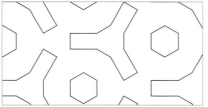

Variations from a Tessellation. Numerous geometric patterns can be derived from an underlying set of lines and shapes. Design: Isabel Uria.

Working the Angles. A triangular grid underlies this digital montage. Small base triangles combine to form larger shapes. Fill colors alternate to create depth. Design: Molly Hawthorne.

WALKER SHOP / GIFTS

Walker Art Center Identity.
Design director: Andrew Blauvelt.

JEWELRY ❈ KIDS ❈ PAPER ❈ GIFTS

Kit of Parts

Designer Andrew Blauvelt uses the term "kit of parts" to refer to his systems-based design methodology. In creating a new identity for the Walker Art Center in Minneapolis, Blauvelt and his design team at the museum constructed an open-ended system rather than a static logotype. They devised a set of ornamental marks that are typed on a keyboard like a digital typeface. The eclectic patterns reflect the Walker's diverse program. The Walker design team can produce endless variations of the system by combining existing elements; they can also add new patterns as needed, creating a living visual brand. Whereas traditional graphic identities are closed systems with fixed rules, this one is open and flexible. Designers can apply this way of thinking to many situations in order to develop a series of genetically related forms. *Ellen Lupton*

"Design itself has broadened from giving form to discrete objects to the creation of systems: designs for making designs."

Andrew Blauvelt

How to Design a Kit of Parts

01   **Create your parts.** The first step is to create the kit. Elements can be built, drawn, or photographed by the designer, or they can be sampled from the existing culture. Designer Kristian Bjornard compiled images of sustainable landscapes using a small number of elements.

02   **Reconfigure.** Determine how to combine your elements. Bjornard found that he could describe different types of trees as well as diverse modes of technology with his elements. He used a simple vocabulary of lines and shapes to generate a richly varied syntax.

Line weights

Shapes

abcdefghijklmn
opqrstuvwxyz
1234567890

Bullets and Leaves (opposite). To create these elegant yet sinister images, the designer rendered leaves, bullets, and arrowheads as both high-contrast silhouettes and as full-color tonal images. She made the floral shapes by rotating and repeating the elements. Design: Virginia Sasser.

Letters and Icons (above). The kit of parts consists of a complete square plus a square sliced into two pieces by the arc of a circle. The designer created a relatively complex alphabet from these simple pieces. He went on to create icons of people and animals as well as flat patterns. Design: Aaron Walser.

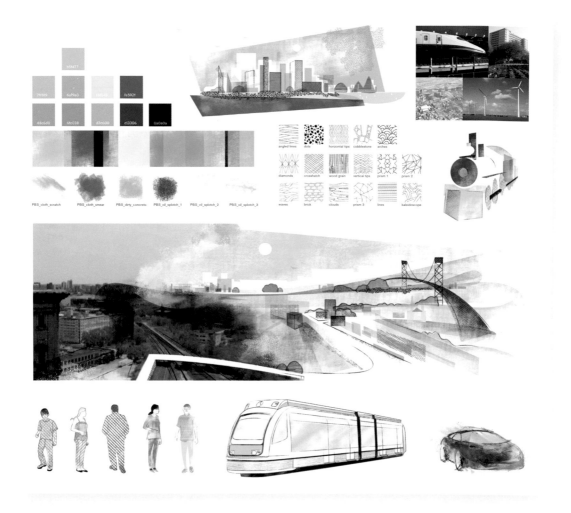

Case Study
Detroit Animation

The designers at the multimedia studio HUSH build tool kits of visual assets that form the basis of complex animations. The kit consists of a palette of colors, textures, shapes, and illustration components.

Blueprint America: Beyond the Motor City. For a PBS documentary about the future of Detroit, HUSH created animations showing how the city might evolve. They combined photographs of the existing city with bright, evocative drawings that convey an optimistic tone.

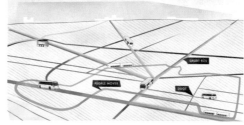

The designers pushed for abstract ideas rather than concrete visualizations: rebirth of city centers depicted with fluid movement, light-rail transportation rendered as flowing particle systems, energy-saving shelters visualized by adding elements to existing structures. The results speak about what could be without trying to predict the future. Creative directors: David Schwarz, Erik Karasyk. Lead producer: Jessica Le. Producer: Tim Nolan. Art director and lead designer: Laura Alejo. Designer: Jodi Terwilleger. 2-D and 3-D animation: Tim Haldeen, Wes Ebelhar, Michael Luckhardt, Marco Di Noia, Andrew Bassett.

Apple Fit. Semitransluscent material with a peek-a-boo die cut creates playful yet alluring packaging for this line of brassieres. The color coding and apple type signify cup size. Design: Tiffany Shih.

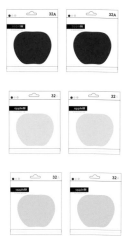

Brand Languages

A brand language is more than a logo. It is a system of design elements, such as color, shape, image, typography, texture, pattern, and materials, created to convey a company's values to a particular audience. The look, feel, and behavior of a brand language can have the power to trigger associations, express values, and inspire loyalty. An effective brand language gains cultural fluency over time, building a conversation with its audience. Tiffany's blue boxes, McDonald's golden arches, and UPS's brown trucks represent visual identities that have benefited from decades of public reinforcement. To create a new language from scratch, designers draw on the communicative power of visual elements and cultural references. *Jennifer Cole Phillips*

For a fresh and relevant book on building brands, see Marty Neumeier, *The Brand Gap: How to Bridge the Distance Between Business Strategy and Design* (Berkeley, CA: New Riders, 2005).

How to Build a Brand Language

01 **Define the audience.** Before deciding what language to use, you need to know who you are speaking to. Identify who will receive or interact with your brand, considering factors such as age, lifestyle, and education.

02 **Create a vocabulary.** Once you are confident about your audience, build a collection of verbal/visual elements that can be applied effectively to vehicles that will deliver the brand messages.

03 **Decide the order.** Emphasize brand elements according to a hierarchy: Which component is most prominent? Least prominent? What are the spatial, scale, color, and compositional values that situate each element inside of a defined order?

04 **Apply systematically.** Establish ways to apply your brand language. Explore how rigid or flexible the rules will be by applying them to different vehicles, such as packages, building signs, uniforms, or tags. Try applying elements in surprising ways such as enlarging scale, wrapping around corners, and bleeding elements off of edges.

05 **Document the family.** Whether you are making a concept presentation to a client or creating a user's manual for a brand language, take care to organize, explain, and document the elements included in the brand family.

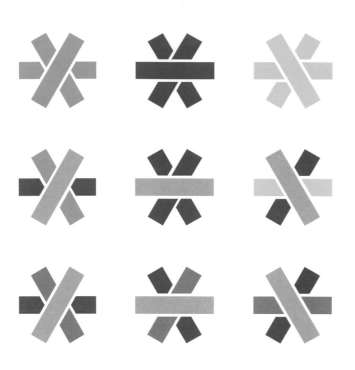

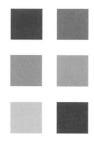

Case Study
FAB

These visual identity proposals for FAB, a public high school for fashion, architecture, and basic design, employ line, shape, color, and form to allude to the design process. Designer Ryan Shelley built a graphic mark out of modular elements, demonstrating a common design method. Supisa Wattanasansanee used wireframe diagrams to suggest structural analysis.

Carried away. The bold application of the mark to stationery, apparel, and portfolios conveys hipness, humor, and visual sophistication. Design: Ryan Shelley.

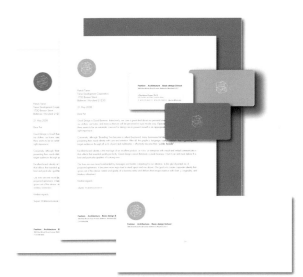

Living Language. Business stationery, bus shelters, and tote bags are just a few vehicles the designer chose to demonstrate how the brand language might live in the world. Design: Supisa Wattanasansanee.

C : 25 M : 30 Y : 65 K : 40	C : 30 M : 00 Y : 20 K : 20

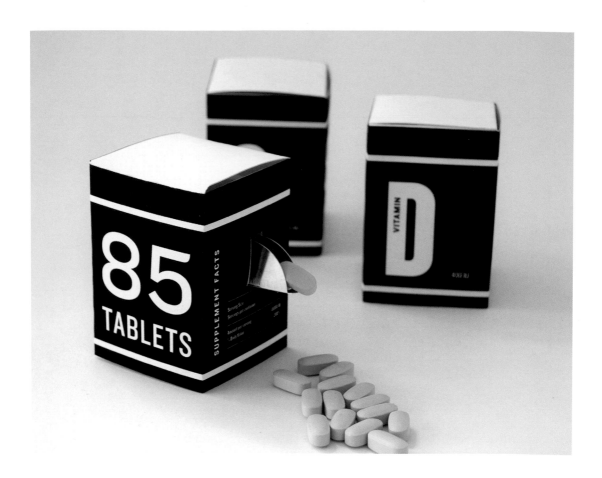

Mock-Ups

A mock-up simulates how a design will look, feel, and behave after it has been printed or produced. A mock-up can be constructed in three dimensions or created graphically with drawings or photographic montages. Mock-ups are tools for exploring the formal and physical properties of applied graphics, such as scale, shape, surface, and hierarchy. Designers create exploratory mock-ups to test materials, proportions, and construction details. Whether simulated in Photoshop or handcrafted with real materials, mock-ups are invaluable tools for testing ideas and communicating to clients. *Jennifer Cole Phillips*

Spouting Vitamins. A classic cardboard Morton's Salt container inspired this packaging prototype for a vitamin brand. To create the mock-up, the designer carefully removed metal spouts from the original salt packages and grafted them into the walls of his own boxes. The flat drawing below was printed, trimmed, and folded to create the 3-D box. Design: James Anderson.

VITAMIN

D

400 IU

85

TABLETS

SUPPLEMENT FACTS

Serving Size | l
Servings per container | 85
Amount per serving | 10000 IU
% Daily Value | 200%

FACTS

Vitamin D is a vitamin that is needed by the retina of the eye in the form of a specific metabolite, the light-absorbing molecule retinal. This molecule is absolutely necessary for both scotopic and color vision. Vitamin D also functions in a very different role, as an irreversibly oxidized form retinoic acid, which is an important hormone-like growth factor for epithelial and other cells.

How to Create a Mock-Up

01 Plan. Find or create a 2-D pattern or plan for what you wish to produce. If you are designing a package, find an example that has the basic shape you want, flatten it out, scan it, and either trace or digitally draw lines for cutting and folding, adjusting the scale and proportion as needed.

02 Design. Apply color, typography, brand marks, and other components to each plane, taking care to place elements so that they will be correctly oriented when your package is folded and built. Make quick sketches and prototypes to check orientation. Print your completed design.

03 Produce. Once you have printed your design onto the paper or material of choice, carefully score all of the lines that indicate folded edges and cut lines defining outer edges. Bend and build the form into three dimensions. Use double-sided tape, gluestick, or basic white glue as needed to stabilize the mock-up.

Ready for a Close Up. Before producing his final prototype, the designer moved through many stages of trial and error to be sure that elements such as typography and composition were thoroughly resolved. Since the project will primarily live in his design portfolio, he also photographed the pieces carefully and professionally.

Case Study
Silver Oak

Designer Ryan Wolper created this elaborate packaging prototype for a boxed edition of special vintage Silver Oak wine bottles. Research about his target demographic of young, upwardly mobile professionals led him to a solution that balanced price and production quality by using smaller bottles but retaining fine attention to detail. In order to mock-up

the sandblasted glass and wood-burned typography, he experimented with a laser cutter until the tonal value, contrast, and fidelity were just right. Chain-hung neck tags and tongue-and-groove box joinery completed the cohesive prototype for this branding project. A polished mock-up like this one makes a strong portfolio piece or an impressive client presentation.

Tulane School of Architecture. The designer created a collage out of layers of paper (left). He photographed the effects of glare (opposite) to enrich the surface of the final poster (far right). Design: Martin Venezky.

Physical Thinking

Designer Martin Venezky creates graphic form by experimenting with the physical properties of materials. This process helps him step away from the computer and produce imagery and typography imbued with depth, imperfection, and accidental qualities. How does a piece of paper wrap around an object? What happens when a length of string falls to the ground? Slowing down the design process and observing physical forms can help designers learn from the nuances of space, light, and texture. Venezky uses this method to make fresh connections between form and content.

During the initial phases of his work, he experiments with physical materials, taking his time to develop concepts through process, rather than letting the concept drive the process. He allows surfaces and structures to speak to the content on their own. By letting the material work for him, he slowly builds the character of each project. *Chris McCampbell*

Martin Venezky documents his creative process in his book *It Is Beautiful...and Then Gone* (New York: Princeton Architectural Press, 2007).

How to Think Physically

01 **Draw.** Starting with some kind of source material (a photograph, a piece of text), explore lines, shapes, and their relationships with each other. Pick out what catches your eye, and make new connections. Don't worry about color yet. Don't try to make clever connections to content. It's okay to be abstract. Be critical of what is working visually and what is not. Experiment in several directions; if something is not working, try something else.

02 **Build.** Experiment by transforming your drawing into a 3-D object by working with paper, cardboard, foil, mesh, or other available materials. Look for materials and objects around you—in the next room or across the street. Ignore nothing, as anything can become inspiration. Study the form of your inspiration, and try to see how it can relate to your drawing. Place pieces together to create interesting patterns, textures, or shapes. Allow things to fall or rearrange themselves. Be accepting of collisions and haphazard groupings.

03 **Photograph.** Explore your creation through the lens of a camera. What can each element say individually? What does the piece say from different angles? Study light and shadow, and observe what changes. When you come in close, the scale of the material can change and become more abstract and universal.

04 **Conceptualize.** Begin to bring content and meaning into your studies. How can the form now communicate meaning? Add pieces that may help to translate this. Start playing with color as well.

05 **Refine.** Bring your elements together into a whole. Think of where you can place and blend elements together.

Case Study
2-D to 3-D Poetry Poster

In a weekend workshop at MICA, Venezky handed out poems written in international scripts; he challenged the designers to respond to the poems without knowing their meaning. The first step was to create drawings inspired by the form of the scripts. Next, the designers translated their drawings into 3-D objects made from everyday materials such as paper, cardboard, and foil. In the example shown here, designer Chris McCampbell, inspired by the ribbonlike forms of Arabic calligraphy, pinned thin strips of paper to the wall to create looping lines in space. He then photographed the objects. Finally, he created a poster that incorporates lines from the translated poem. Following this unusual creative path yielded unexpected results.

الوحيد الذي أعرفه

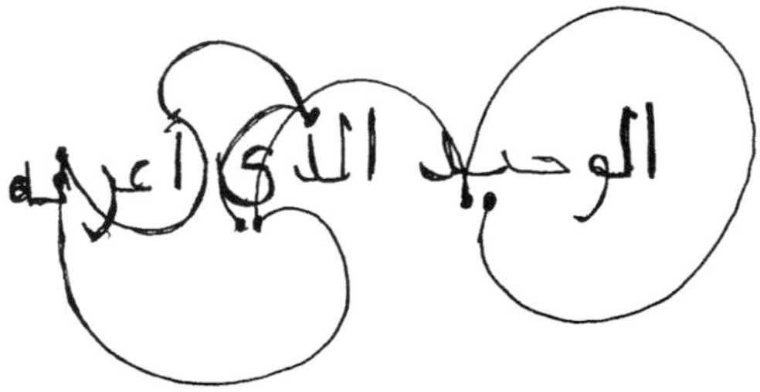

الوحيد الذي أعرفه

Complaining is Silly. Stefan Sagmeister mobilized environmental forces to create this billboard. He laid stencils on top of newsprint on the roof of his New York City home/office. The exposed areas yellowed in the sun. As more sunlight hit the billboard, the message faded.

Take the Matter Outside

Blow off the cobwebs. If your work feels stagnant and stale, try exposing it to the physical environment. This technique encourages exploration of cities, suburbs, rural farmland, your own backyard, or any setting in between. Consider ways to find, implement, and test the relationship of your medium of choice to the great outdoors. Formulate scenarios, arrange encounters, conduct experiments, or search haphazardly. How can you redirect the medium by following and/or breaking the laws of nature? The natural environment provides an accessible tool for generating authenticity. Basing design thinking on visceral encounters helps "keep it real" in an otherwise digital world. *Elizabeth Anne Herrmann*

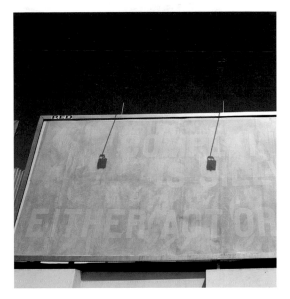 

How to Take the Matter Outside

01 Texture. Ask yourself about the physical qualities of printed media, from the support (paper, wood, Plexiglas, cardboard) to the manner in which it is marked (inks, relief, die cuts, stickers, cut vinyl). What happens when these components encounter the natural elements? Use decomposition to create texture. Employ texture to enrich printed, digital, and motion-based work.

02 Climate catalysts. Employ weather conditions to catalyze change in your ingredients. Rain, wind, slush, ice, humidity, or the sweltering sun offer possibilities of entropic design by natural processes.

Observe naturally occurring relationships and sequences. How do plants and animals instinctually transform under changing conditions? Observe the physical effects of time, climate, and pollution on outside surfaces. For example, vinyl, a cheap and commonly used signage material, doesn't fare well outdoors for long periods of time. You can view this as a detriment or appreciate its disturbing beauty.

03 Projection. For motion graphics, try playing your clips outdoors. Study the effects of combining other sources of natural and man-made light with yours.

What happens when a video sequence is projected onto unexpected surfaces—different textures, intersecting planes—or at odd angles and distances? What happens when you remake the piece in the venue where it originated? Try projecting a video sequence or photograph in the same place where the material was initially recorded—and shoot the projected scene. Explore how the medium and content of your design reconfigure because of the environment.

Climate Studies. Feel the a-peel. Let the climate do the work. Observe how surfaces rust over time. Look at how salt and grime smog up a windshield. Peer into a gutter to see your own reflection after a rainstorm. Experiment with how climate can change your own work in progress. Piece together new compositions from images of an environment breaking down. Photography and design: Elizabeth Anne Herrmann.

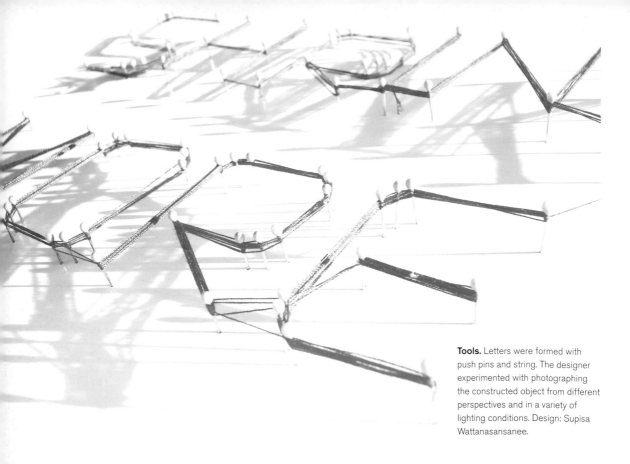

Tools. Letters were formed with push pins and string. The designer experimented with photographing the constructed object from different perspectives and in a variety of lighting conditions. Design: Supisa Wattanasansanee.

Unconventional Tools

Designers often put their ideas to paper in ways that feel comfortable and familiar—usually with pen, pencil, or computer. Standard tools often produce standard results. The most efficient mode of producing ideas may not yield inspiring approaches. Using different tools—by changing the way we physically render our concepts—can end up loosening the constraints set by our own habits and expectations. The complex personalities of tools can push ideas beyond the ordinary. Brittle materials, like tape and wire, will resist your hand and add their own voice to a drawing. A peeled potato is a harmony of organic and geometric form. Deflated balloons have a beautiful sadness. Like physics or chemistry, good design can synthesize perfect ideas with the imperfect world they live in. *Christopher Clark*

Draw it like you're messed up.

How to Use Unconventional Tools

01 Decide what forms you want to create. A logo might call for a circle or square. A layout might need typography that is rough and naive. Perhaps a poster requires something that looks vaguely like a keyboard or the head of Marilyn Monroe. Keep your concept phase simple. The wonder of materials is their ability to pick up our mental slack.

02 Put down your pencil and step away from the computer. (Unless you plan to operate the mouse with your foot.)

03 Find some marking tools. Try a stick from the backyard and some India ink or a hammer dipped in paint. Think of these components abstractly. For example, your marking tool might be a grid of pins fixed with red thread. After you've done it once, do it again. Put yourself at the mercy of your tools.

04 Choose wisely. Once you've tried different materials, choose drawings that balance form and function, beauty and clarity.

05 Make it graphic. Use your drawings to make marks suitable for communication. Translate your work into a medium that can be reproduced. You might create a vector path based on a line drawn with a shovel, or photograph pebbles arranged on a page.

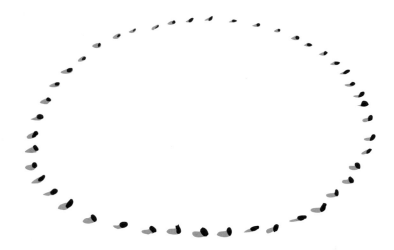

HEARTLAND EGGS

Case Study
Heartland Eggs

In this logo study for a fictional egg farmer, designer Christopher Clark employed unusual drawing processes to invent new forms, breathing an unpredictable sensibility into applied design work. His exploratory drawing process yielded a series of simple, spontaneous marks. His drawing instruments include a hammer and ink, acrylic paint and a box cutter, a camera and furniture, white tape on a studio floor, and basil seeds and paper. Clark chose the last experiment for its organic shape and subtle dimensionality.

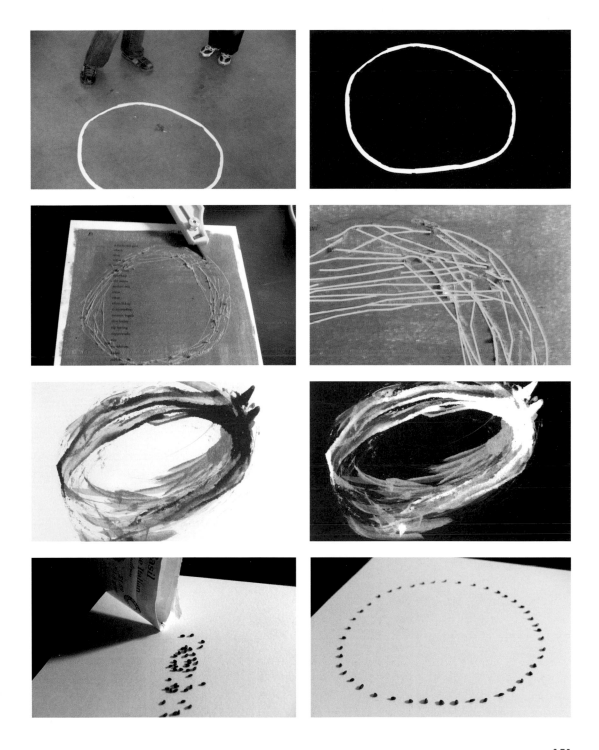

Case Study
Tracing with Toilet Paper

This project was part of a course taught by Pongtorn Hiranpruek at the Alliance Française in Bangkok. The course is open to the public, so many students are new to the visual arts. They lack drawing skills and are unfamiliar with software. This tracing and drawing technique helped nondesigners generate visual images and learn how to use digital tools. First, they traced images onto toilet paper, leaving space between the drawings. Then they used markers to add color to their pencil outlines, allowing the ink to bleed through onto a piece of paper placed beneath the tissue. They scanned these blotted color images and digitally traced them with Illustrator to make vector graphics. The icons were screen-printed onto shirts.

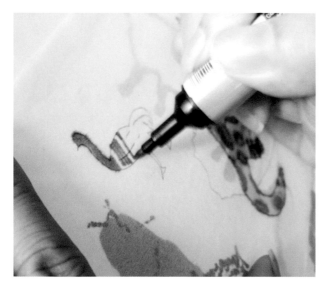

Case Study
Making Letters

Typography and letterforms can be put together or taken apart using unconventional tools, from folded paper to a photocopy machine.

Build. The progression of this *e* demonstrates its process of construction using ink, tape, paper, whiteout, and a photocopy machine. Pieces have been cut apart and reassembled, composed and decomposed. Design: Elizabeth Anne Herrmann.

Folded-paper Letters. The outlines of the alphabet were created by folding 2 x 2 inch squares of paper. Design: Isabel Uria.

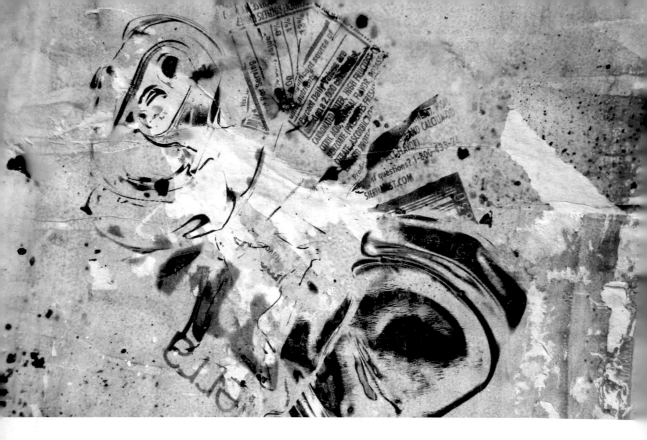

Regurgitation

Design doesn't always happen at your computer. If you have been sitting in your chair for too long, it's time to get up and make a mess. If your work is starting to resemble three-week-old cottage cheese, try this technique for expelling that sour smell. Regurgitation is a process for turning moldy iconographies into something fresh. Use it to restore vital materiality to familiar visual languages. Make many iterations, and make a mess. From the mass and the mess, you can come away with fresh ways of looking at commonplace artifacts. Begin the process with open-ended exploration, and end it with ruthless editing. Images produced this way can become fodder for logos, identities, illustrations, or the pure visual substance of T-shirts or posters. Learn the how behind constructing meaning as you shift connotations and excavate personality from experimentation. Regurgitate: out with the new. *Elizabeth Anne Herrmann*

Does your work resemble three-week-old cottage cheese?

Crushed Coke Can. The regurgitation process extracts unanticipated forms from discarded objects. Design: Elizabeth Anne Herrmann.

How to Regurgitate

01 Take a walk. Bring along a plastic bag, camera, and sketchbook. Collect weathered ephemeral matter you find discarded on the streets, especially printed materials. Choose an artifact that has text on it, such as a broken bike wheel, a handwritten narrative, a parking ticket, a sign, an aerosol can, or scraps of cardboard.

02 Study it. What is it? What is it made of? What is it capable of doing? Of becoming? Explore its materiality and function.

03 Restrict yourself. Using just this one artifact, reconsider and recompose. Do what you know how to do, what you don't know how to do, and what needs to be done. Break down the object physically. Demonstrate its essence: If it has none, give it some. If it has too much, take some away. Mess around with the parts. For example, if you drive a monster truck and it has an interesting tread pattern, you could use that texture to change the surface of a Coke can. Shapes transform and letterforms torque, creating new and unexpected imagery.

04 Document. Using a digital camera and/or pen and paper, document the recomposed artifact. Consider environment, lighting, depth of field, and how the object is displayed. Your means of translation could mean anything from putting the artifact on a pedestal to shooting it against a green screen.

05 Splice and dice. Photocopy the drawings/photographs and your notes. Bump up the contrast, manipulate the images as the light moves across the glass, photocopy them onto previously photocopied papers, and more. Cut out parts from one print and collage them with others. Play with paper and ink. Get out a pair of scissors and a glue stick. Make at least fifty renditions. Don't count. But have fun.

Case Study
Decanstruction

Elizabeth Anne Herrmann collected dozens of crushed
soda cans. Her photographic studies yielded imagery
for a screen-printed poster.

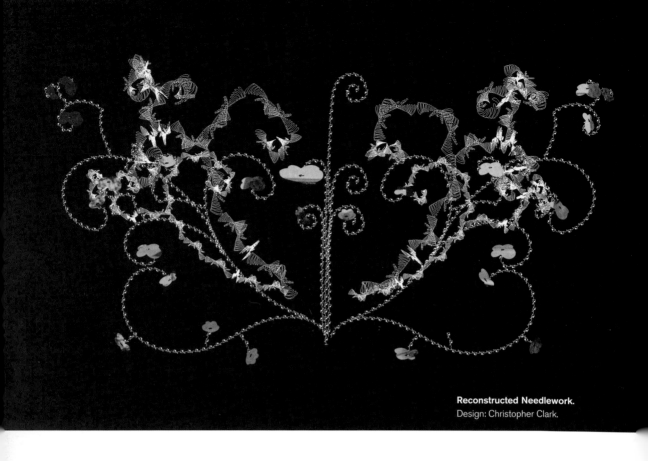

Reconstructed Needlework.
Design: Christopher Clark.

Reconstruction

Finding inspiration is easy. Translating it into your own language is a challenge. Collecting intriguing artifacts takes time and a sharp eye, but only hard work and careful thought can harness their expressive powers. Visual language has its own logic. Things look the way they do because of thought processes buried within them. A crossword puzzle does not look like a crossword puzzle unless the placement of black squares favors the right and bottom sides. This is because word lengths are limited from the right hand side and never the left. The texture of a nineteenth-century needlework drawing is limited by the number of stitches available and the fabrics on hand. Learn to study visual languages and implement them for new purposes in new media. The task is to dissect it, see its logic, and reconstruct it. *Christopher Clark*

Images have a language that can be learned and spoken like any other.

Crossword Logic. Creating crossword-puzzle typography is harder than one might expect. An even dispersion of black and white squares reads only as a checkerboard, not a crossword. The visual language of a crossword puzzle conforms to the length and direction of words in a given language. The numbering system also plays a subtle yet critical role in the unmistakable patterning ot this graphic genre. Design: Christopher Clark.

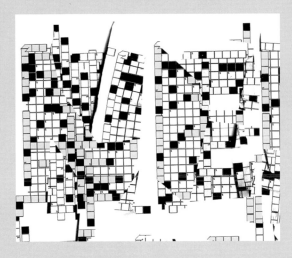
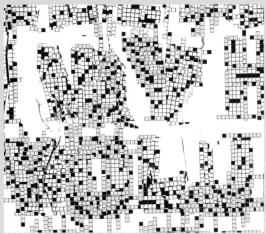

How to Reconstruct

01 Collect source material. Choose your inspiration actively: Renaissance paintings, sixteenth-century clocks, or the poetry of Walt Whitman. Find what moves you.

02 Analyze and replicate your sources. If you want to know how a clock works, take it apart. The same thing applies to style. Understanding why something looks a certain way comes from unpacking it and playing with its elements.

03 Observe. As you analyze your sources, you will begin to notice how their means of construction make them look the way they do. Take note of the details and study their origins.

04 Compile a dictionary of elements. If you were learning German or Chinese, you would study a word list. Likewise, designers can learn by building collections of shapes and marks. Use your list as a graphic vocabulary sheet.

05 Make your own images. Now that you understand a grammar and vocabulary, start constructing new sentences on your own. Draw lines and shapes based on those in your source material, but communicate your own vision and ideas. As you gain fluency in your new language, the potential becomes endless.

Case Study
Folk Art Studies

Designer Christopher Clark began his process by studying embroideries from the eighteenth and nineteenth centuries as well as traditional quilt patterns. He created an illustrative graphic style based on forms observed in the embroideries. After sketching the historic pieces, he built dictionaries of marks that he could translate into digital illustrations. The resulting pieces are graphic and contemporary yet harbor the naive delicacy of the source material.

Folk Art Sources (clockwise from upper left).

Artist unidentfied. South Hadley, Massachusetts, 1807. Watercolor, pencil, ink, silk thread, metallic thread, and chenille thread on silk and velvet with printed paper label. 17 in. diam. American Folk Art Museum, Eva and Morris Feld Folk Art Acquisition Fund, 1981.12.8.

Sallie Hathaway (1782–1851). Probably Massachusetts or New York, ca. 1794. Silk on silk. 17 x 20¼ in. American Folk Art Museum, promised gift of Ralph Esmerian, P1.2001.284.

Artist unidentified. New England or New York, 1815–1825. Wool with wool embroidery. 100 x 84 in. American Folk Art Museum, gift of Ralph Esmerian, 1995.32.1.

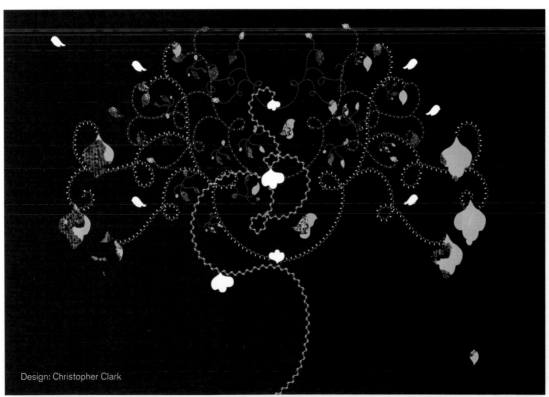

Design: Christopher Clark

Not Like Grandma. Here, traditional quilting patterns have nourished visual imagery that is both graphic and ripe with personal voice. In these reconstructed illustrations, complex patterns nest within simple shapes to re-create a crafted vocabulary. The shape and color palettes were inspired by memories of family quilts made by grandmothers, great aunts, and church quilting circles. Design: Christopher Clark.

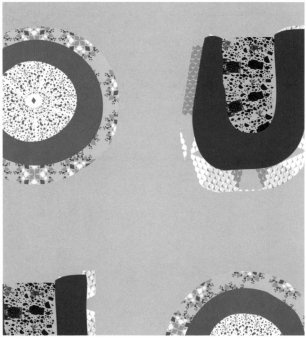

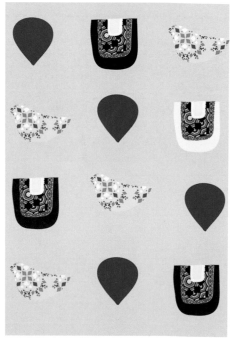

Elizabeth Anne Herrmann
asked over a dozen designers
to describe their work process.

How Designers Think

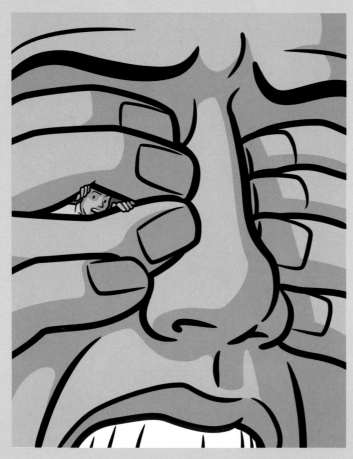

Illustration: Christoph Niemann

So you have a design project. You look at it. It looks back at you. With the time you two spend together, a relationship forms. And sometimes it's hard to get started at all. Here, designers share tips and techniques for getting in the mood to get ideas.

How Do You Get in the Mood?

Christoph Niemann

An intriguing idea looks effortless. Unfortunately, I have discovered that the quality of a concept is more or less proportional to the effort and agony that goes into it. Hence the question, how do I get in the mood to have ideas? is terribly close to the question, how do I get in the mood to do push-ups?

I can't have any music or any distraction. It doesn't help to look at any reference material or find inspiration in books and magazines. I just sit at my table and stare at a piece of paper. Some ideas come easier than others, but I am a bit disappointed that even after years of working, this process hasn't become any more jolly.

The one thing that makes doing push-ups more agonizing than thinking of ideas is that with the latter I can at least drink coffee.

Abbott Miller

I get ideas by talking about a project. When you can talk with someone else, you can build on each other's observations and arrive somewhere that neither person anticipated.

Bruce Willen

I don't think there's such a thing as a technique for getting ideas, so I'll just talk about a key principle: collaboration. This is one of the most important elements of the creative process. Working with another person can bring outside perspectives and diverse ideas and opinions that aren't possible working on one's own. Even just having a friendly ear as a sounding board can help distill one's thoughts and make it easier to separate the wheat from the chaff.

Carin Goldberg

I usually work on insanely short deadlines, so there is no time to get into any kind of mood other than a bad one. Usually, I panic and go into idea overdrive. I sketch like crazy until something clicks, and then I work like a maniac until I design something I'm happy with. I keep a sketchbook next to my bed and often wake up in the middle of the night to frantically capture an idea. I like to keep the TV on while working. The din of inane banter keeps me calm and focused.

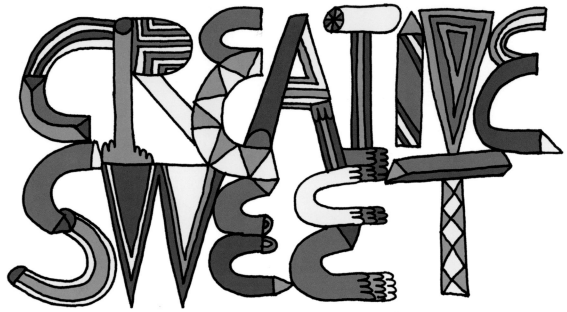

Design: Mike Perry

Mike Perry

I just vomit out work. It comes naturally and in abundant amounts.

Kimberly Elam

True creativity is unpredictable. Snippets of ideas come at odd hours in mysterious ways. These ideas are fleeting, so I always try to have something to write with so I can jot down notions, quick thoughts, or a satisfying combination of words. It's impossible to tell when suddenly something interesting will appear that begs for more investigation.

Don't underestimate the mind/body connection. Things such as refreshing sleep and strenuous exercise provide a relief from more cerebral pursuits. Getting away from the stress of creativity-on-demand helps reset the cycle. If creativity was easy, everyone would be doing it.

Paula Scher

Ideas come in all kinds of ways and at different times. I get them waking up in the morning, or in a taxi, or in the midst of a conversation, or at a museum. I seem to get my best ideas when I am not trying to have an idea but am involved in something else. If I am blocked and unable to come up with an idea, the best thing I can do is distract myself. Going to the movies works.

Maira Kalman

I don't have design ideas. I have deadlines. And a deadline usually gets me in the mood for illustration and writing. But I spend a lot of time wandering around, traveling, and looking at everything: people, architecture, art. I read books and listen to music. Thoughts and interests are bouncing around all the time. To really get in the mood, I take a walk. That usually provides plenty of inspiration.

AFRIQUE CONTEM- PORAINE

Design: Philippe Apeloig

Philippe Apeloig

The inspiration for ideas, posters, and typographic compositions comes from many different aspects of my personal life. I live in the center of Paris in a very busy district, and I am constantly surrounded by noise from the streets and people. Even the dirt and grime add elements and layers.

For me, every project is different. I combine elements from contemporary dance, architecture, literature, and photography. I also spend a lot of time in museum exhibitions looking at different art forms. When beginning to create something new, at first I spend much of my time looking at interesting new typefaces and shapes. Doodling and drawing are all a part of my process. Drawing comes directly from myself and later informs what I do on the computer.

When I begin a poster, I lay out construction lines that will serve as support for the text. Most of the time,

I start from a text, from typography, and I continue with images. I use the editing techniques from film editing: I carve my ideas into pieces and then reassemble them in a different order. I manipulate them until the composition is right and strong enough to fix itself in the visual memory of the public.

The development of ideas is a very complex labyrinth. In addition to the pertinence of the concept, I take into consideration the structure of the page. In the next step, I break up the rigidity of my composition. I like it when a poster gives the illusion of movement. There must be an impression of spontaneity, even if the result is really a product that has been precisely and minutely detailed. I also dislike working with known quantities, those that are already ossified. This explains my constant hesitation, my temptation to do and redo things.

Dear,

This letter is to say that it is over between you and me. I'm so sorry I have to tell you this now. But don't take it personal. I hope we will stay friends.

For some time I have believed, like you, that we would stay together forever. This is over now. Some things you shouldn't try to push. but just leave as they are...

As I find writing this letter very & painful I won't make it too long. I don't have so much time either, because tonight (friday 25 february 2000) I'm going to the preview of a new show by Mattijs van den Bosch, Ronald Cornelissen, Gerrit-Jan Fukkink, Connie Groenewegen, Yvonne van der Griendt, Hine Kramer, Marc Nagtzaam, Désirée Palmen, Wouter van Riessen, Ben Schot and Thom Vink, 8 PM. I think it is at 1e Pijnackerstraat 100; I forgot the exact address, but I'll see.

Mattijs, Ronald, Gerrit-Jan, Connie, Yvonne, Hine, Marc, Désirée, Wouter, Ben and Thom are all great friends of mine. We will probably go out afterwards.

But this doesn't mean that I don't care about you. I have to go. I'm already late.

▶

ROOM invite 210x297 mm
recycled letter

goodbye

1e Pijnackerstraat 100
NL 3035 GV Rotterdam
T/F 010 2651859
T/F 010 4773880
E roombase@luna.nl

friday / saturday / sunday
1 — 5 PM

ROOM organized by
roos campman / eric campman /
karin de jong / ewoud van rijn
ROEM organized by terry van druten
ROOM thanks to PWS Woningstichting

Design: Maureen Mooren and Daniel van der Velden

Perhaps you lie on your back and stare at the ceiling imagining the dots and cracks coming together to make a shaggy dog licking a dead rat. Or maybe you take a trip to a distant land and observe native peoples grind ruffage for a medicinal tourniquet. Inventing form is unique to everyone. Whether it's drawing, shooting, cutting, pasting, or smearing around some chicken blood, we each give it our own spin.

How Do You Create Form?

Daniel van der Velden

I'll talk about form by describing a specific project I did: an invitation for ROOM, an underground gallery started and run by friends. In exchange for creative freedom (unlimited but committed), I did these invites for them for a few years. I am still very happy about the series, which was conceived as a set of half-fictional letters containing real information.

The idea for the invitations originated with me sifting through some hilarious—with hindsight—letters I'd written or received around the age of seventeen. Handwritten letters from girls sometimes had these big dots on the i's and j's. I thought it would be an interesting idea to write a typical adolescent letter in the style of a Dear John correspondence, which is the ultimate rejection letter, and then make that the invite. I wrote the text on a computer and a friend of mine, Vanessa van Dam—herself a graphic designer—did the handwriting, adding big circles as dots on the i's and j's. The idea was that any recipient of the letter would basically feel like a seventeen-year-old receiving a handwritten letter of rejection, while the hypothetical girl-sender who'd written it would have this enormous number of friends, the artists exhibiting their work.

The idea about form is that the handwriting should convey a mood, one that Vanessa caught brilliantly! Even in an age of deteriorating handwriting and Facebook, the written letter still evokes some of that mystery of a desirable someone who is losing interest, pulling back while pretending to still care. I'm not saying that was what I experienced at the time, but that was the overall mood—an omnipresent yes and no.

Art Chantry

Geez, after six-plus years of higher education and thirty-five-plus years in the field, I have yet to figure out what the word *form* means. It's one of those words that is in common use in academic circles that I think really doesn't mean anything. It's sort of a word that gets tossed around to sound important and intellectual but is totally vapid. Form is an abstract concept with no basis in reality.

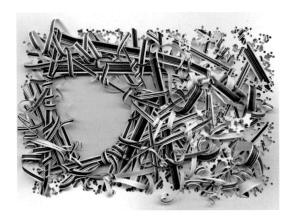

Design: Martin Venezky

Design: Jonathan Barnbrook

Martin Venezky

I teach a class, Form Studio, at California College of the Arts, which is the first studio class that all our grad students take. A decent description of the class can be found in my book *It Is Beautiful…Then Gone*. The principles I developed for the class are the same ones I use in my own practice.

I like to begin with materials and engage their properties. I have a storeroom of materials, tools, and drawing implements on hand to play with. As the results develop, I try to invent properties for the elements. The trick is to try and make the work feel like it designed itself out of its own inner logic rather than having a form imposed on it by a designer. Like plants that are growing in a garden rather than flowers that are arranged in a vase.

Louise Sandhaus

How do I invent form? Hmmm. I noodle around, mostly! I belong to the form-allows-function school of thought, so first I identify the problem the design is solving, and then I work toward making something that looks as wonderful and engaging as it is meaningful. I start with images of things that already

delight me, and then I use these images as a starting place. I just play and play with my own approach and often with collaborators to get something that works. Working with collaborators forces me to articulate what I'm thinking. Conversation and noodling. Those are my secrets.

Jonathan Barnbrook

Form comes first from a new ideology or philosophy. It very rarely can appear by just working or visually experimenting. Form has to be absolutely about the meaning of the work—what I am trying to say and the most interesting way to say it. Visual novelty is almost a distasteful consequence.

In fact, I am very cynical as to the role of new form in graphic design. Yes, there is always the need to re-create and reinterpret the world anew for each generation: it's a basic human need. However, we also have to look at how this new form is immediately appropriated. Offered up as novelty in order to sell people exactly the same thing over and over again. Designers should be smarter, aware of how their creative need gets used, if only so that they can be more careful about how they let it be used.

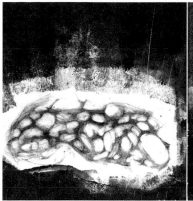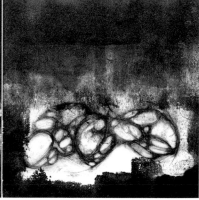

Monoprints: Jessica Helfand

Jessica Helfand

I am answering this question while spending ten weeks in Rome in a studio with pencils and paper and wire and clay and oil paint and acrylic paint and a digital camera. I have no agenda—other than the fact that I am working in a new and unfamiliar way. Well, not entirely unfamiliar, as I have been painting for nearly a decade but not in circumstances such as these. I have stripped down everything contextual about visual form and have gone back to the beginning: the line.

How do you define a line? Where does it start? Where does it go? And if indeed it does go somewhere, when does it stop being a line and become something else? When does it represent flat space, and when and how does it go from a 2-D to 3-D representation of that space? What if it breaks or shifts or migrates or deviates into something else? And at what point do we perceive that line as something more than a mere abstraction?

The line remains for me the most elemental, fundamental component in making form. For one week, I made studies in color that loosely referenced the colors I had witnessed in India earlier this winter

(2010)—bold and vivid, unusual (read "clashworthy") combinations that I painted methodically, illuminating the gaps between them by approaching the empty space with a paintbrush. Knowing that I have spent most of my adult life at Yale, a visitor came in one day and shrugged. "Guess you had to get Albers out of your system," she said. Albers, I probably don't have to tell you, held absolutely no role in this exercise.

This brought up another point about making form: do we need to copy others, modeling ourselves on their example, in order to achieve recognition? While I delight in looking at things in books and in museums, I don't personally feel this is how one should approach time in the studio. Philip Guston wrote brilliantly about this syndrome—about all the "voices" in your head that you have to get rid of before you can do real work. I recall this quote from him: "What kind of work would you be doing if you thought no one was looking? Do that work."

Doyald Young

First off, I think it's impossible to clearly answer this question. You must first define form. Form may be defined as dependent on the artist's aesthetic.

Design: Keetra Dean Dixon and JK Keller

In the vernacular, if the artist can't draw well and has lousy taste, his form will be ugly. If you want to delve philosophically into the subject, read George Santayana's *The Sense of Beauty* (1896), which he later said was hogwash. Or ask yourself what makes you think one object is more beautiful than another. Or more ugly, depending on the desired effect. Why are John Singer Sargeant's portraits elegant, breathtakingly beautiful?

As for my abilities, all that I ever try to do is to draw a 2-D object as carefully as I can. The outcome is dependent on what I think is beautiful. There are many, many horrendously ugly fonts. What makes them ugly? So, I really haven't answered your question. Except I can say that every Marc Jacobs design is bone-deep ugly. And forget that it's camp.

Keetra Dean Dixon

I routinely practice formal thinking-through-making exercises, or material explorations with no assigned outcome. This allows room to discover the unexpected. One example of this process, which I applied digitally with the help of my husband, JK Keller, is what I call digital tool breaking: using digital applications in ways they weren't meant to be used. We often partner Javascript with Illustrator to push existing effects and filters beyond what would occur via typical use.

My other favorite formal exploration method uses process. I often set up a system of rules to treat certain material and let that system play out over a period of time without intervening. Then I utilize/edit the outcome. I recently used this process to create a typographic sculpture. JK and I applied thin layers of wax to build 3-D letterforms, repeating the layering process dozens of times for a month.

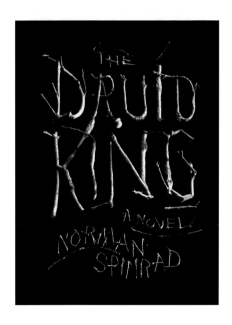

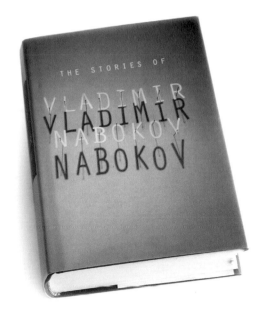

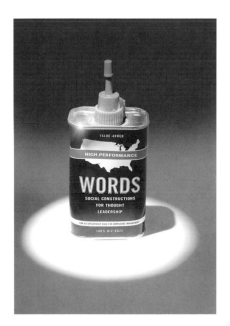

Design: Stephen Doyle

Stephen Doyle

I don't honestly know how to answer such an open-ended question, short of writing a book. But I would rather cut up other people's books than write my own. I start out by thinking about language. Not type, not letterforms, but words, because they are so very abstract—symbols for sounds that get strung together until they make one collective sound that represents a thing or idea. Then I try to think if there is a way that that word can enter into the real world, where all things cast shadows and have physical properties. I like to imbue these abstract things with properties that make them part of the world we see. But that's not how I make form, that's how I think about projects or create work for myself. When I think about form, I often just start by folding paper. And sometimes the paper has words on it.

FRÉMONT PEAK ST. PARK, San Benito County, California, March 6, 2008

Approximate *Location* of the **INCIDENT AT**·····················

GAVILÁN

── PEAK ──

WHERE **UNITED STATES FORCES** RAISED THE AMERICAN FLAG,
DISOBEYING MEXICAN AUTHORITIES ON **MARCH 6TH 1846**

★ *California's*
HISTORICAL LANDMARK
No. 181

HISTORIA No. 1
NUMBER ONE IN A SERIES
OF 13 LABELS

HISTORIA No. 13
NUMBER THIRTEEN IN A SERIES
OF 13 UNIQUE LABELS

⊩ **CAMPO DE CAHUENGA** ⊩

NORTH HOLLYWOOD

LOS ANGELES COUNTY, CALIFORNIA,
JAN. 13TH, 2007

3919
LANKERSHIM BLVD.

LOCATION
for the signing of the

Treaty of **Cahuenga**

BETWEEN THE **UNITED STATES** OF **AMERICA** AND **MEXICO**

ENDING HOSTILITIES IN *Alta California*
SIGNED BY CAPT. JOHN C. FRÉMONT AND GOVERNOR ANDRÉS PICO ON

JANUARY 13TH, 1847

★ *California's*
HISTORICAL LANDMARK
No. 151

Design: Rudy VanderLans, Emigre

Perhaps your strength lies in making—and making lots. Are you guilty of presenting fifty-page PDFs overflowing with renditions? If so, you may get overwhelmed by the sheer quantity of variations you create. Choose something. Making choices is key to a successful outcome.

How Do You Edit?

Rudy VanderLans

Your question made me think of a story told by Ira Glass about how aspiring designers start recognizing good design long before they learn how to make good design. (He was talking about writing, but it applies to all art.) There's no shortcut to getting from recognizing good design to actually making it. It requires practice, and it requires a lot of editing, and you get better at it over time. If you're lucky, you'll never really get there, because if you do, you're probably not challenging yourself.

Recently, I've been working on a very involved type specimen book, and I've been thinking about the issue of editing as I'm working. I can honestly say that I cannot describe the process that goes on in my mind. It turns out that the decision-making process I utilize is a complete mystery to me. Not trying to come up with a smart answer simply because the question needs answering is a form of editing as well.

Obviously, design equals editing. When I design something, I work on it until it makes sense and looks good—and until any further change made to it makes it less so. The longer I work this way, the more difficult it becomes. It's a constant search to recognize what comes naturally to you, the ability to express those feelings honestly without being distracted by what is currently in style, while knowing fully well what is in style. When I stick with all that, I may end up with something that looks halfway decent.

David Barringer

How do I edit? I dream. I improvise. I fail and try again. If you are an adherent to a particular ism (modernism, postmodernism, realism, the International Style, De Stijl, Paul Randianism, the Bauhaus, whatever), you have solved with one stroke of your sword the Gordian knot of editorial judgment. In other words, you abdicate your judgment in favor of strict rules. You still have to apply those general rules to your specific design (the way lawyers apply the law to specific cases), but you don't question the rules.

As for myself, I don't follow an ism. Which means I am not just the lawyer and the judge, I am also the legislator and the philosopher. I can change the rules.

Design: David Barringer

I can change policy. I can change the whole system of governance, as it applies to my current design project. This can be liberating and empowering, but it can also be a real pain. It can be a lot of work. I can become ambivalent. I can paralyze myself with indecision.

So I have many tricks and strategies and lines of thinking. I will limit myself here to the design of book covers. For book covers, I strive to represent some part of the content of the book, be it mood, tone, genre, a character's perspective, setting, or something else. That gets me started. Then I fool around with ways to limit myself. Because the rules have not been written, and the tools are wide open (I can use an ax to chop wood into type or I can paint on my chest or, you know, on and on), I have to find some way to limit myself. These limitations can be drawn from the book's content. Let's say abstract and black-and-white and all handmade. Or literal photography and collage and left-justified type. Or cartoonish and garish color and warped perspectives. These limitations enable me to move toward a mood or style or point of view.

Practical concerns help limit the horizon of possibility, which for me stretches as far as the mind can conceive, forward and backward in time. So once I've messed around with seeking limitations, I see what I have left. What other criteria can I use to get me started? Sometimes it's something as simple as whim. I feel like using a photo. Or I feel like trying something I've never done before, like making type out of braided bread for a murder mystery about a baker who strangles his victims.

That playful phase of seeking out forms inspired by content and seeking out limitations in tools and perspectives and practical concerns will end soon enough, and I've got to crank out some covers. It's after this period of concentrated work that I sit back and review the three or thirty-five covers that I've done for the book. Variations on a theme, on a mood, on a tool, on a perspective. Now I have to edit. I have to cull the herd.

This is tough and yet not so tough. If nothing jumps out at me as perfect, then I realize none of them will work. If there were thirty covers, it's likely because I regarded every one as a failure and kept creating cover after cover. But even if there are only five covers, I can reject any cover for any reason and end up with a cover that is unobjectionable—and bland, boring, and blah.

The best designs connect to the subject matter, the content: they are not literal but figurative; they can sustain more than one interpretation. They make you want to pick up the book and look at the cover, but they also reward you when you have finished the book and return to look at the cover. These are all conclusions about a design. They are qualities of a final design. They are not practical rules for making editorial judgments, really. Knowing the qualities of the final design doesn't help me get there. It's like I can see the foggy outlines of the mountain in the distance, but that doesn't help me determine the best way to get there. I need to go through all the work I described above to get there, and I may still end up at a different mountain—or in a different fog.

Basically? I dream.

Erik Spiekermann

When we are involved in developing the strategy for a project, we determine a set of values to judge our work by, summarized in a set of not-too-redundant adjectives. (Everybody wants to be dynamic and user-centric, so these adjectives are not so useful anymore.) We measure our work against these criteria, always asking, is the result what the brand requires? Recently, the rebranding for a chain of supermarkets that carries a large range of organic products was grounded around the adjectives "meaningful, alive, simple, genuine." Those are useful criteria for a graphic designer to work with. The result won't be black-and-white grids.

If no criteria are provided by the client, we make our own. To establish benchmarks, we look at what the competition is doing, and the position we see the client in, their present design style, their ambitions, but also their capabilities (which often are two different things). In the end, our experience tells us how much pain the client will take and how big the gap is between what they think they want and what we think they need. It is often better to ignore the client's brief and come back with a set of tough questions. Sometimes that ends the project; sometimes it starts a relationship.

Georgianna Stout

On some of our bigger branding projects, we conduct studiowide charettes, which allow for designers of all levels and areas of expertise to sketch logo ideas. These often yield walls full of concepts—some viable, some not. Often there are real surprises, things that we wouldn't have thought of or allowed to develop if we had been working within a more controlled sketching process. We usually discuss and decide as a group how to narrow them down to a more manageable set that we can refine and post again. I usually edit down to a set of ideas that seem to resonate with the content first and foremost as well as those solutions that are graphically strong. I guess it's a kind of internal knowledge (as you say, a gut instinct) of what you think will work well for that particular client, along with a desire to always include ideas that seem unexpected and new.

Ivan Chermayeff

The only criteria for choosing a design is excellence. The chosen solution must be appropriate, original, distinctive, and, if possible, simple and easy to reproduce. It must also be adaptable to different

Design: Luba Lukova

media, perhaps requiring alternate versions for color or other requirements.

The most important part of the process of design is not to accept any direction easily. Editing means rejection, rejection, rejection—never stopping until you have something really good. This solves the problem in question. Never accept bad or only adequate.

The next problem is just as difficult—figuring out how to get a design accepted and to convey how a design is to be used.

Luba Lukova

I always do a lot of research by reading and absorbing visual information. Then I try to distill what I've learned and begin making preliminary sketches. I love that part of the creative process, and I try to extend it as long as possible. Usually, my first idea is the best. When I really like the theme of my project, such as a poster for a Shakespeare play, I push myself to explore more possibilities, even if I'm sure that my first idea is going to work, just for the pure joy of immersing myself in the text.

Ken Barber

When it comes to editing, I let the project brief guide my decisions. Sticking to the job outline makes it easier to determine whether the work exhibits a clear purpose, conceptual integrity, and aesthetic appeal. If the work in question satisfies these requirements while responding to the demands of its application and the needs of the client, then the vetting process practically takes care of itself. For me, this process isn't exactly a conscious one, but rather an internal dialogue that I have formulated over years of practice.

My editing process is very personal. It involves all of my intuition and logical thinking. I keep an archive of good sketches that have not been used, because they can often trigger an idea for another project. In that sense, the work process is more important than the finished piece because I've learned new things that can be helpful in the future.

When I discuss my ideas with a client, I usually show about three sketches; most of the time my clients agree with my choice. If I know the client well, I sometimes show them my entire sketchbook. But I rarely do that, because I'm afraid that can be disorienting. A couple of times, I've shown just one

HOUSE INDUSTRIES
GIRARD SLAB NARROW LIGHT

BEST·L·TT·IN
WEST BARNUM

CX CHAMPIONSHIP
GIRARD SKY

J. Irwin Miller House
GIRARD SLAB REGULAR MEDIUM OBLIQUE

AIRWAY
GIRARD SKY

Alexander Girard
GIRARD SLAB HEAVY

Columbus, Indiana
GIRARD SLAB REGULAR MEDIUM

SANTA FE
GIRARD SLAB WIDE LIGHT

Typefaces designed by Ben Kiel, House Industries; West Barnum designed by David West/Photo-Lettering; digitized by Ben Kiel

solution in an almost finished form, and it has worked out fine. On those occasions I've felt that my idea is right, and there is no need to distract the client with additional choices. When I meet with clients, I try to be a diplomat and make them feel that their own choice coincides with mine. But I'm also always doubtful about my work, and sometimes I ask the cleaning lady in my building to tell me what she thinks. If she understands what I'm trying to say, then I know that I'm on the right path.

Ben Kiel

I'm a typeface designer, and the dirty truth about typeface design is that the design bit is about 5 percent of a project. The other 95 percent is the production of that 5 percent. This means that there are really two modes of editing: one for the first 5 percent and one for the other 95 percent.

The first editing mode takes the form of research, investigation, and sketching. The first question that one asks is, what is this typeface going to do? The answer to that question guides the editing process. One starts with a vague idea of what is needed, informed by a client, a use, or a thought. Researching

ways that the problem may have been solved in the past and sketching forms is the first bit of editing—though it's really the gathering stage.

To edit all of that down, I start playing with ideas. Often I'll use tools to explore the possible design space—things like interpolated versions of trial fonts (using Superpolator) to find out things like how high/low/wide/tall/open should an ascender/descender/serif/counter be. The goal here is to find the limits of the design space that I am working in. Knowing what won't work is just as important (if not more so) than knowing what will work. I am constantly referring back to the intended use to judge which variations are working. This is an iterative process, trying things and rejecting or combining them until a good working model emerges for how the face should be.

I usually just do this on control characters, so that I don't have to draw everything to test. In short, this phase of editing is experimental, where I throw everything that might work at a wall to see what sticks. The end result is a tight brief for how I want things to work and look. Taking that brief into the next part is the stage when the rubber hits the road and production begins. I draw everything else for the type family with this defined model in mind. Editing here is akin to looking at the blueprint and rejecting things that don't fit the mold. The blueprint doesn't spell everything out, so things have to fit the spirit of the plan, but they need not rigidly conform.

Steven Heller

Let's be clear about what you mean by editing:

1. As a designer: selecting and self-analyzing the best or worst solutions to problems.
2. As a writer: revising text to flow and parse well.
3. As an editor: commissioning, selecting, and critiquing other people's copy.

The first type of editing is something I haven't done for a while. But when designing pages, I would always give myself two or three options. Like playing a child's game, I move elements around until I'm content with the outcome.

The second mode of editing is a process of writing, cutting, moving, writing some more. It's similar to designing. The words and sentences are elements of the puzzle as well. I see words as blocks of type.

The third kind of editing is often the easiest. I can see what someone else has done that is, say, overindulgent, underwritten, or sloppily constructed. I can remove, add, and recompose if necessary. Usually, I trust a good writer to produce a good story. Then it's a matter of whether I want to publish it or not.

I do not develop specific criteria in a conscious manner. I adhere to certain habits, but I try to be open to new approaches. Usually, I follow my gut.

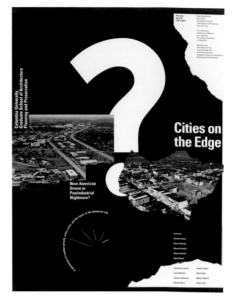

Design: Willi Kunz for Columbia University, Graduate School of Architecture, Planning and Preservation

Willi Kunz

By the time of editing, each of my designs has passed through three phases: concept sketch, preliminary design, and comprehensive design. Consequently, at the end of this process, I am familiar with the strengths and weaknesses of each design, and I am able to gauge whether or not it meets the client's expectations. At this point, the fitness of a design to solve a particular problem is clear to me, and the choice is more or less obvious.

After selecting the final candidate, I pick an alternative in case of an unpredictable client who has different ideas and goals. I always make sure that this runner-up is compatible with my first choice, in case the client likes some aspects of both—a rare worst-case scenario.

When editing reaches a dead end, I consult with my wife, who is not a designer. Her critique is illuminating, but in the end, I follow my own instincts.

Index